Books by Donna Bocks

Lavender Blues
Came to Say Good-bye
Heartbeat of Home
Purple Prairie Schooner
Texas Tango
Twin Trees

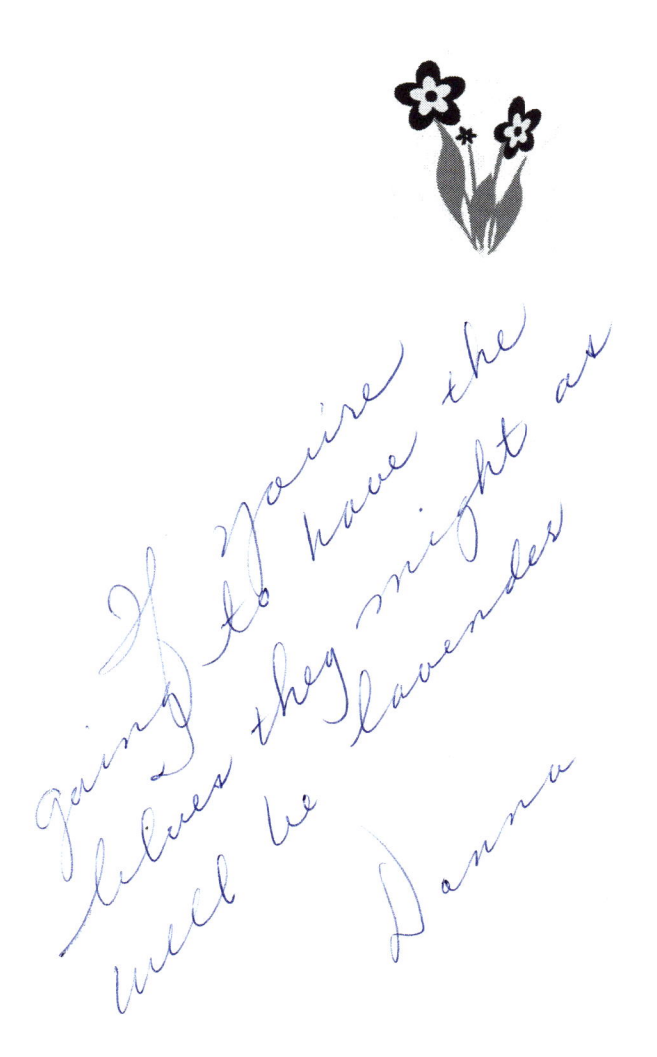

I hope you're going to have the lilies they might as well be lavender

Donna

Donna Bocks

Lavender Blues
By Donna Bocks

Published by Open Window Creations

Donna Bocks, P. O Box 8231, Holland, Michigan 49422-8231.
DonnaBocks@birthAbook.com

ISBN: Lavender Blues: 978-0-9802090-4-4
Project Development: *Open Window Creations*
Cover and Book Design: *Greystroke Creative*
Printed in the United States of America

Copies of this book may be ordered from:
www.lulu.com
DonnaBocks@birthAbook.com

Acknowledgments

How does a 78 year-old get the desire and courage to finally bring her six typewriter-written novels out of the basement, and into the hands of a reader? By reaching out for lots of support!

In the beginning, I was a writer of stories, and received encouragement, feedback, and knowledge from Donna Winters, Dennis Hensley, the Writers Digest School, the Midwest Writers Workshop, and the Herrick District Library Writers Group. Thank you!

In June 2009, I attended a workshop facilitated by Patricia Lynn Reilly, Publishing Coach and so much more. She challenged me to bring my six novels out of the basement and into the hands of a team that produced the book you're holding in your hands! Many thanks to her team of editors, designers, and assistants.

Throughout the years, I've been mother, grandmother, and friend, and my family and friends have supported me, unconditionally. A special thanks to my children and their spouses who joined Patricia's team to illustrate, digitize, and read the typewritten manuscripts on their way into your hands.

Each word in the novel you're reading, expresses my thanks…

For Sadie

 CHAPTER 1

Why were Sally and Charlotte laughing? It really wasn't appropriate. The farther they walked, the more out of control they became. Reactions to death took mysterious forms.

"Poor planning on Samuel's part. January, indeed." Sally nodded in agreement as the umbrella leaked.

A nasty whirling wind lifted Sally's hat. They chased after it, rescuing the wet piece of felt from flopping into a muddy puddle.

They hadn't realized how miserable the weather had become. One smart move was they had worn boots. When they arrived at the cemetery gate, the laughter vanished.

They had walked because they had felt that if they didn't get some fresh air in their lungs they'd suffocate. Besides, it was only a short distance from Charlotte's house.

Samuel had requested that the service be a brief graveside ceremony. He'd completed arrangements months earlier. Sally's chest tightened, but the frigid air cleared her mind. She wished Samuel had not left so soon.

The few car doors closed with subdued respect. Sally glanced over the small crowd. Paul, Samuel's nursery manager, was in attendance. A few men who were probably business friends were there, plus a few personal friends whom Sally didn't know.

She looked back toward Paul again and didn't know how to react to the way he was staring at her. He made her feel like she had no right being there. She felt intimidated whenever he was in her presence. Looking away quickly, she tried to forget about him. This was not the time for such feelings.

Dark clouds became darker, and freezing rain was pelting heavy coats.

The two women couldn't concentrate on the short message that the minister delivered. Each was thinking her own thoughts.

At the conclusion, an elderly gentleman stopped next to Sally and handed her a business card. Tipping his hat, he said simply, "You must call me." Looking puzzled, Sally smiled faintly and slid it into her pocket.

Several people offered them rides, but Sally and Charlotte refused politely. No condolences were exchanged.

All hurried to their cars and back to their busy lives. Sally wondered if anyone who was there cared about Samuel, or had those few moments been a formality? Dear, sweet Samuel! There were many things I would have liked to talk to him about.

Three cemetery employees stood back from the plot waiting to cover the grave.

"We should leave, Charlotte," whispered Sally.

Charlotte paused then spoke, "Would you grant me a request? Would you hold my hand as we leave?"

When Sally turned, she was surprised. What a state Charlotte was in. Her eyes told a sad story, and her cheeks were glistening with tears that must have been collecting for far too long.

Sally wrapped her arm around Charlotte's shoulder. Pulling the umbrella closer to their heads, she tilted it forward to protect them as much as possible.

They sloshed back toward Charlotte's house in silence. Sally guided Charlotte through the whipping foliage. It felt like they were being shoved through a freezing car wash.

Charlotte had left a light on in her kitchen which gave a ray of cheerfulness to the dismal day. She cleared her throat and steadied her voice as they closed the door on the wet wind.

"Come, we'll get warm. I've laid out tea and homemade bread and jam. It was Samuel's favorite."

They removed their coats, hanging them to dry.

Charlotte began to shudder, less from the cold dampness than from a flood of emotions. Her hands flew to her face, and she couldn't stop the flow of tears.

Sally suggested that she sit on one of the kitchen chairs. She found a blanket folded on the end of the sofa and bundled it securely around Charlotte.

She turned the burner on under the tea kettle and finished setting the table. Then she moved a kitchen chair next to Charlotte and tenderly reached for her hand.

When the tea kettle began to whistle, they looked at each other and smiled.

As Sally poured the tea, she winked at Charlotte. She wasn't sure how to handle a situation like this. "Enough of that blubbering, Miss Charlotte. Life must go on. Samuel would not approve of such carryings-on." She paused a moment.

"Did you make this bread, Charlotte?"

"Yes, he enjoyed it so."

Sally reached across the table. As she touched Charlotte's hand, she asked, "Would you like to tell me about it?"

Charlotte sat back in her chair. Releasing a deep sigh, she said, "I loved him." Squeezing her eyes shut, she then relaxed and reopened them. "I have never said those words out loud."

"Do you think he knew?"

There was silence for a few minutes, and then Charlotte continued. "I don't think his heart would have been able to give up the love he had for your aunt. It was buried very deeply inside. Maybe I would have been able to give enough to encircle both of us." She got up to pull a tissue from the container on the counter top. "I shall miss him dearly. I treasured his company."

"He spoke often of your kindness after he became ill," said Sally. "What was the reason for his plot being back in the corner by itself? It seemed like that area was not kept up as well."

After a sip of tea, Charlotte answered, "I asked the funeral director about that. He said Samuel chose that because it was an out-of-the-way spot. He had said he wanted his resting place to be in a quiet area so he could die as he lived. He said he didn't want folks walking all over him. The director added that the gravestone had been prepared all but for the date and year, 2002, so that it would be placed soon."

After Sally had put away the food and wiped the table, she turned to Charlotte. "Will you be okay alone tonight? I need to get on home, lots of work to catch up on tomorrow. They were kind at the bank to let me have the time off for my aunt's funeral. I'll stop by after work."

"Bless you. I'll have supper ready."

Sally began to protest, but the idea seemed to bring so much delight to Charlotte's face that she thought better of it. Charlotte was so used to doing for others that she was lost unless someone needed her.

 CHAPTER 2

At 7:30 the following morning, Sally let herself in the side door of the bank. She was proud of the nameplate on her desk: Sally Gordon, Branch Manager. Yes, it was the smallest division, but she was pleased with her accomplishment.

It was her freckles and red hair combined with a winning smile and mischievous eyes that caused people to think she was still a girl. Though she was thirty, it was difficult to conceal her youthful enthusiasm. She was able to give the impression of confidence and professionalism. Still, Sally felt a self-imposed pressure to prove her qualifications for the managerial position.

She'd been that route before. Others believed in her abilities, and so did she, to a point. Then she'd slam into that invisible barrier. Sally could feel it close around her. It was a passing emotion that nagged at her, but why? She scowled, and then recalled her Aunt Violet's advice. "Don't ignore the things you don't understand; sort them out, think them through, then move on. You waste valuable time worrying about nothing. You have talents beyond what you can imagine. Go get 'em."

Sally missed her aunt. There were no more understanding words of wisdom.

With that thought, she pushed her chair away from her desk. Rising, she stood tall, promising herself that there would be no more invisible walls to slow her down.

Heading into the main part of the bank, she greeted the other employees who had arrived. Her smile was radiant. No more hesitation would be allowed. She would shine, not only for herself but so her aunt would be proud.

Sally had returned to her hometown, Green Bay, following four years at college. She accepted a position in the loan department of a bank there. Gradually she worked her way up to department head.

Her life had been moving at a smooth pace. Too smooth; the excitement of challenge had waned.

Testing her wings last March was what had produced the major change in her life. With a "no harm in trying" attitude, she had sent her credentials for the bank manager position in Greenbriar.

Within three weeks, she had moved her belongings to a furnished apartment in Greenbriar, Michigan. The town was adjacent to Block Lake and Lake Michigan. Word had it that the summer resorters were like firecrackers compared to the locals.

Returning to her desk, Sally knew she should be concentrating on bank business. Instead, she was recalling the day in mid-March when her Aunt Violet called her from the nursing home. She had been so excited. "Hurry, dear. I'm having a good day. There's something important I need you to do."

Knowing Violet's memory recall did not last long, Sally had hopped in her car and sped across town.

Violet had acted like she was sharing a secret. She spoke hurriedly. "I've been told you are moving to Greenbriar, Michigan. Go to the edge of town, by the water where the two lakes join. Look for manicured woods. The spring flowers will look like blue carpeting. If he's still there, tell him . . . I've never forgotten."

With that Violet stared out the window and was lost in the past. Sally kissed her on the cheek and drove thoughtfully back to work, wondering what Violet could have meant.

The thought was soon lost in Sally's scramble to move and get settled.

Sally's adjustment to her new job was swift, and it had given her staff an added feeling of compatibility. Each of them offered tidbits of information about Greenbriar. One thing that pleased Sally was hearing about the many bike paths.

In the beginning of April, she took her bike from the rack in the garage. No matter that she had to bundle up; it was time to become more familiar with the roadways and people without being enclosed in her car. Between her walking and her biking, she felt her muscles firming up. The warmth of spring was slowly moving in.

Returning to her apartment on a sunny Saturday in April, she had found a packet of mail from home. On the bottom of the pile was a letter postmarked from Lansing, Michigan. Who could it be from?

Ripping it open, she checked the signature. Tim! How could she have forgotten his handwriting? The two of them had kept in touch occasionally, but the contact was slowly severed. College friends—there were lots of them, but six had stuck together like a club. There had been four girls and two guys. They had all been in different programs, and Sally couldn't remember how the bunch of them got together.

Come to think of it, now that Samuel was gone, some of those precious memories had slipped away also. Sally had been so grateful for his friendship.

Sally sat on the sofa and eagerly began to read Tim's letter.

April, 2001

Sal,

I'm sending this to your folks' address. It's been too long. What's happening with you these days? After using my business degree to provide a few coins for my livelihood, I've landed a job in Lansing. I'm an assistant to a prominent horticulturist (my second degree). Actually, we work for the state in a scientific capacity. We travel to areas with problems, studying different types of growth, soil, etc. Remember the words you had taped on your desk at college? "I am still learning, Michelangelo." Am I ever! I don't think a day goes by that I don't write extensive information in my notebook. Love to hear from you. Return address on the envelope. No phone at the moment. Snail mail only, sorry. When I'm at home I prefer peace and quiet. If not busy with work, I try to catch a game at State to relax my brain a little. Please write.

    Tim

Ignoring the rest of the contents of the envelope from Wisconsin, Sally sat down with her writing tablet. She invited Tim to come over for a day. He would be surprised to see how close they now lived to each other. A new job, new town, and an old friendship renewed. She was elated.

A few days later Sally's answering machine had a message from Tim asking if he could come by next Saturday. He had left his work number.

In her call back, Sally gave her okay to a secretary. Seemingly familiar with the situation, the accommodating voice promised to pass the word along.

 CHAPTER 3

On that Saturday in April, a car with a noisy muffler had pulled into Sally's driveway. The driver climbed out, double checking the house numbers to make sure he was in the right place.

Sally observed the familiar face that never had looked clean shaven and the prominent Adam's apple. His hair was windblown, and a barber appointment was overdue.

When Tim raised his head and saw her in the upstairs window, his wonderful grin took over. It forced his eyes to squint and those big creases to engulf his face.

Good ol' Tim! Sally raced down the steps. They exchanged an exuberant hug.

Eager to show off her new place, Sally trotted up the stairs ahead of him. As they stepped through the doorway of her apartment, Tim let loose a sigh.

"This looks great, just like you. My place looks sloppy in comparison." He shrugged his shoulders and grinned. "I did shave this morning. Today, it was visit you or get a haircut."

Sally laughed. "Don't apologize. You look like you always did. If you showed up all spit and polish, I wouldn't have recognized you. It's great to see you, Tim. You look so . . . healthy—it must be nice to work outdoors."

"It's great. This is a job I like. Before this, I worked in Detroit as an accountant, and then for a technology firm in Dallas. The money was much better, but I discovered I didn't care for the city."

He sat quietly for a minute then continued, "So, I pulled out; took my time getting back to the area where I'd come from. I heard about this job and hurried to apply. The man I work with cares about people and the environment. I feel like I count for something."

"Come on now, you never were a country boy," Sally teased. She told him about her position at the bank back home. "There were some changes after being away for four years, but there wasn't the adjustment you had. Some of my former classmates had returned home to work also, and we managed to get together quite often. You know, a few good movies, a few dull dates." Sally wrinkled her nose and laughed. "I needed an all-around change; job, friends, territory. This opportunity was an answer to all of those. Now we know the old stuff, what's new?"

Tim said, "All of a sudden I missed our group from college. I had something to share and no one to share it with."

It was then Sally remembered that Tim's family had been lost in a boating tragedy during his senior year in high school.

"See, I've finally got myself, sort of, a girlfriend. You talked to her."

"The secretary?" Sally had never seen Tim blush. She couldn't help but laugh. "That's great, Tim. Tell me about her."

"I got to know Mary through work, and we've been seeing each other for a while. She's shorter than me, has blond hair and blue eyes and . . ." His sentence floated off into space. Sally didn't have enough of a picture yet but obviously Tim could see the image clearly.

Feeling she should respond, Sally said, "She sounds nice."

Tim seemed thoughtful. "I hadn't considered describing her. I just feel

. . . comfortable around her. She had other plans or I'd have brought her along so you could meet her. I told her I'd try to be home in time to take her to a movie."

Sally replied, "Aw, I was thinking of tying you up and keeping you here for weeks. Oh well, you've spoiled my plans. I had figured that I'd show you around, but it has just dawned on me that I don't know much about the town." She frowned to herself as she realized that even with her walking and biking she'd covered little territory. "As I've been here about a month between adjusting to new surroundings and the job . . . I might not be the best guide."

Tim said, "Come on, we'll check it out together."

They went tooling around town, Sally with her fingers crossed hoping the police wouldn't pull them over for noise pollution. Maybe the muffler had been put on hold—like the haircut.

Sally's head was on a swivel. New to her was the tiny vintage clothing store, and next to that Jungle Jim's Java Joint. That caught Tim's eye and he swung into a parking spot.

"My stomach is crying for food. Let's eat."

Upon entering, someone called from the back, "Seat yourself, folks. Menu's on the chalkboard." Tim and Sally took a table by the window, ordering iced tea, ham and cheese sandwiches, and a bag of chips to share.

After lunch, Sally directed Tim to the bank. Using her key, she took him in to see her office. The maintenance man was running the polishing machine across the lobby floor.

Tim spun Sally's leather desk chair around, acting serious as he seated himself. "Well, Miss Gordon, I'm impressed. I didn't picture you in the banking business. Are you happy, Sally?"

Sally was surprised by his question. Before she could answer, he had jumped to his feet and taken her arm. "I need to head for home."

She knew she should get him back to the apartment so he could be on his way. For a second she didn't want him to leave.

While backing out, he rolled the window down and yelled over the noise, "This was great! Let's do it again before too long."

"Sounds good!" She shouted, waving as his car rumbled away. As much as she liked the idea, Sally doubted if he would make time to come by much now that he had a girlfriend. But she felt privileged that he had shared his news with her. His visit had reminded her of a couple of things: they had shared more laughter than conversation, and a social life was what made things tick. "Sally girl, you've been neglecting some important stuff."

It wasn't four o'clock yet. Still feeling carefree, Sally decided to take a bike ride to finish off the day. Lifting her bike from the rack, she headed out. Three blocks away, workers were preparing ground for a new high school. She stopped to study the architects' rendering of the finished product that was posted by the corner. She suddenly realized how weary she was.

Lying in bed that night, she mulled over the past few weeks. The settling-in process had been accomplished. It was time to throw in some leisure and social life to complete the picture.

It rained two days straight after that. On the third day, the sun picked her spirits up again. After work, Sally took the bike path that headed along Lake Michigan to the town north of Greenbriar.

There was a breeze, and the whisper of the pines was like a lullaby. Sally paused to talk with a woman walking her dog. She explained to Sally why the pine smell was so strong. It seemed that the pines along this scenic ride were being trimmed and some of them cut down. Storms that blew across the lake had wreaked havoc on the trees and power lines. There would be fewer power outages, but they agreed that the barren look would take some getting used to.

As she rode on, Sally suddenly remembered her aunt's strange request. She decided to set aside the following Saturday for an investigative ride to see if she could solve the mystery of the manicured woods.

So, on the last Saturday in April, Sally made sure she was free for the day. Stopping at a small park for swallows of her bottled water, she had a chat with some serious riders. They were talking about lengthy rides they were signed up for in the summer. It was obvious their equipment was top-of-the-line and so was their clothing. She felt out of place with them and was not sorry when they pushed on.

She felt much more comfortable when a lady in jeans and a sweatshirt pulled up next to her. They were each locking their bikes so they could use the park restroom. Sally spoke up. "Those guys are serious, huh?"

The woman smiled. "You're not kidding, but there are plenty of us who ride for the fun of it. We aren't speed demons and some of our equipment is losing its luster. Some of us are, too." They shared a laugh.

Sally's new friend dug around in her fanny pack and came up with a piece of scratch paper and a stub of a pencil. "My name's Susan. I'll be glad to give you my phone number. If you need spur of the moment company on a leisure ride, give me a call sometime. I can also give you information on a couple of local clubs that ride for fresh air and friendship.

"They're a mixed bunch, all ages and interests. Are you new in the area?"

"Yes, I am. It sounds like a great way to meet people."

As Susan was preparing to move on, Sally remembered her aunt and asked for directions to where the two lakes joined.

She chastised herself for not trying to find this secret place earlier. It had seemed so important to Aunt Violet. Susan waved as she peddled away.

Sally headed north and soon found herself rolling past stately homes surrounded by lovely flower gardens. Most of them had fancy wooden signs with unique emblems identifying "their place."

Eventually, she found an entrance to a dirt roadway. The mailboxes along the main road were banged up from years of wear, and the wooden poles were rotting out. Sally caught a glimpse of the water. This would be as good a start as any.

There were probably dozens of these unpaved roads. It was difficult to handle the bike. Sally surmised that the potholes were deterrents for uninvited guests. Getting off and walking the bike would be easier.

The road ended at an ornate iron gate that stood open enough for a person to slip through. Between overgrown hedgerows, she could make out the outlines of distant buildings.

Leaning her bike against a tree, she felt impelled to move through the opening. What lay before her could only be described as "manicured woods."

Her first surprise was the stillness. The hedges cut off any wind. The protected area provided tranquility as Sally could feel the hustle and bustle of everyday leave her body. It was like a well-planned park; truly a sight to behold. She wished she had thought to bring her camera.

There were some small trees, shrubs, mowed grass, and pathways. Much of the ground was covered with flowers: blue violets, myrtle, and every imaginable blue spring flower hugged the ground. Her timing was perfect: everything was in bloom. Looking up at the blue sky and down at the flowers, she saw one was a reflection of the other. Bending down on one knee, she ran her hands back and forth through the blue carpet.

Then Sally stopped, thinking she could get into trouble trespassing. Before she could stand, just inches from her fingers, she saw a pair of wet leather slippers and droopy socks covering swollen ankles. She took a deep breath as she scanned upward. His pants were too big, and a worn belt with new punch holes was drawn tight to hold them up. Brown wrinkled hands were partially covered with the sleeves of a faded shirt; some buttons were missing.

Sally slowly raised her head to look into a kindly dark face framed by white tufts of hair.

Sally wondered if he could hear her heart thumping. She felt like a scared rabbit. A meek sound came out of her mouth. "Hi."

"Good afternoon, and who might you be?"

Hurriedly Sally stood. "My name is Sally Gordon and my Aunt Violet asked me to hunt for a place and a person. . . . It's obvious that I have located the place." Sally stopped there. What about the other half of the puzzle?

Sally hadn't noticed the cane before. The old gentleman staggered toward a stump and tried to sit down. Sally rushed to his side. "Are you all right, Sir?" He had closed his eyes and sat for a few moments, motioning with his hand that he was okay.

"Your Aunt Violet?"

"Yes, you see she asked me to look for land where the two lakes meet. To find manicured woods where the flowers blossomed like carpeting. And, um . . . to tell someone, if he was still there . . . that she had never forgotten."

The man's eyes remained closed, but tears rolled down his cheeks.

Sally gently placed her hands on top of his. "That's all I know, Sir. My aunt has Alzheimer's, and that's all she was able to tell me."

He looked up at her with deep watery eyes. "I'm so sorry to hear that. When you see her again, tell her I received the message, and that I too will never forget." He shook his head and mumbled, "Things change and we all get older." Then he raised his voice again. "You can't imagine what this means to me. You just can't imagine." With that he struggled to stand.

"So, you are the person the message was for?"

"Yes, and I'm pleased that you are the messenger. Is this your aunt by marriage then?"

"Yes, she is my favorite aunt. Sometimes she remembers things, and sometimes it seems like she is in another world. I have no clue what this is all about. But I do have a general question."

He loved a young person with a curious mind. "Ask away."

"Did you plant all of these flowers? Everything here is so . . . perfect."

He smiled. "I planted some. During the years the birds, bees, and butterflies did most of the work. They visited the surrounding woods then continued to improve on my lawn." His eyes took inventory of the setting. "I've let too many things slide into disrepair these past few years. But this is kept up by my friends at the nursery. Soon they will move the birdbaths into place, and several benches. I'm a bit partial to stumps myself. They complain that it ruins the effect. Then I have to remind them it's my yard. I can be tough when I have to." He laughed and gave her a quick wink.

Who was this man? Why did he and Aunt Violet know each other? Sally could hear the waves of the big lake in the distance. For a fleeting moment life stood still.

Sally turned her head and discovered that the man was studying her.

"I need to get back to the house. I am extremely tired and I must rest. Can we talk again soon? I need to know so much more. You rode your bike? Of course you did, just like she did that day. We must talk. Could you come by next Saturday at this time? I'm sure Charlotte will be happy to make us up a light lunch."

Sally smiled. "I'd be delighted."

He grabbed her hand. "One o'clock then."

Starting toward the house, he turned back toward Sally. "My name is Samuel Mansfield. Just call me Samuel. I shall look forward to seeing you again, Sally."

Turning again, Samuel laid his hand upon his heart. "Oh my dear Violet, how has this come about?"

Once inside, he put on dry socks and sat in his old green chair. Raising the foot rest, he pulled up a warm purple blanket with a large V sewn in the corner and was instantly asleep.

If Samuel had looked out the window, he would have wondered why his visitor remained in the same spot where they had parted.

Sally knew the polite thing would be to gather her bike and leave. Instead she stood very still. Her mind was traveling down many paths. A list of questions was forming. Would Samuel provide answers?

CHAPTER 4

The past couple of weeks had been exciting. First the visit from Tim, then meeting Samuel. It was Samuel's face that kept appearing in her subconscious. Her curiosity could hardly be contained.

Thank goodness tomorrow was Saturday. It wasn't supposed to rain, so she could ride her bike again.

Hoping her expectations were not too high, Sally headed for the lake.

Upon entering the gate, she got off and walked her bike. Immediately that peaceful feeling enveloped her. No wonder her aunt remembered this serene landscape. It was intoxicating.

Off to her right was what had been a gate house or gardener's cottage. It was the size of an overgrown playhouse. Some of the window panes were broken, and the building needed to be scraped and painted. Sally moved close enough to see that the door was held by one screw in the top rusty hinge. It would be snooping to look inside.

When she turned the bend in the drive, she paused. In its day this house must have been beautiful.

Huge double doors gave the main entrance an appearance of formality. Sally imagined a butler in livery answering, asking her name and excusing himself while he announced her arrival to the master or mistress.

Returning, he would escort her into a grand room to await her wealthy host. Sally knew her imagination was working overtime, but just in case, she followed a sidewalk to what appeared to be a service entrance.

There was a small bell mounted by the door. She timidly swung the chain, but the bell clanged loudly.

"Hello! You must be Sally. Park your bike and come on in." A cheerful, plump woman in a calico apron held the door open. "I'm Charlotte."

The kitchen was bright and warm. Sally inhaled aromas that reminded her of home. Charlotte was removing cookies from the oven. Her face was flushed, her green eyes sparkled, and her short brown hair was in ringlets. Sally thought Charlotte was like a pixie wind-up doll. She was on the move and so delightful.

"Samuel hasn't been this excited for a long time. You've given him a reason to perk up. Have a seat at the table. He seldom goes out these days and never was one to invite folks in."

Charlotte's bustling around the kitchen put a smile on Sally's face. After cleaning up splatters on the stove, Charlotte sat down, wiping her hands on her apron.

"Do you live here at the house?" Sally inquired.

"Dear me, no, I live next door. Come, we'll do a short tour."

Sally was allowed a quick look in the living room and shown the guest bathroom. As they passed through the formal dining room, Charlotte lowered her voice. "Very soon Samuel is going to adapt this for his sleeping quarters. This house is so large; there are too many stairs."

She turned to Sally with a smile. Then with pride she opened an engraved heavy wooden door. Its elegance was enhanced by its shine and the lemon smell. Charlotte said with a soft voice, "This is where he spends his waking hours. He'll be with you shortly."

As Sally stepped onto the Persian rug, the door clicked shut behind her.

Sally had never seen a library like the one she was standing in. Across the front, a picture window framed a living scene of Lake Michigan. Flanking the window and lining the remaining walls were heavy wooden bookshelves filled to capacity.

There was a stone fireplace with kindling set up waiting for a match, and nearby a pile of dry firewood.

One wall had books from floor to ceiling. Hooked onto a runner close to the ceiling was something Sally couldn't resist: a ladder with rollers on the floor.

That's where Samuel found her. She was up near the top, pulling herself along so she could see the titles of the old classics.

His soft slippers muted his entrance. He watched her with charmed amusement as she muttered to herself, naming the authors.

"You will get dusty up there." His voice surprised Sally and she clung to the ladder. Since she was looking down, he appeared much shorter and thinner than when she'd met him the week before. She was disturbed by the image. She blushed. "I have always wanted to climb on one of these."

"Well, you must come down, young lady, because Charlotte has told me that lunch is ready. There are two comfortable chairs here, and she is going to bring in a small table. You can climb the ladder another time, I promise."

After making her way down the ladder, Sally took Samuel's arm, and he escorted her to an overstuffed chair that faced the window. He then moved to the one that was his favorite.

"You're not always this formal, I hope."

"No, but this is a special occasion. I have a charming visitor."

There was a knock on the door. Charlotte pushed a serving cart between the chairs.

She lifted the lid of an antique tureen painted with delicate groups of roses, releasing the delicious aroma Sally had noticed in the kitchen. The cream soup had large chunks of chicken with fresh vegetables adding color. In a basket covered with a decorative towel, warm biscuits waited for butter and raspberry jam.

Sally dished up the soup in brightly colored bowls and placed each on a tray.

They ate in silence, mesmerized by the lake's rhythmic motion.

Charlotte entered and began to clear the dishes. Sally stood, saying, "Let me help."

"Maybe next time. Today you are a guest." Sally felt warm inside. She had hoped this would not be a one-time visit.

Shortly, Charlotte returned with a teapot. There was a dainty cup and saucer for Sally. Samuel's was poured into a mug. The delicate butter cookies tasted as good as they had smelled.

Samuel remained silent, contemplating. This niece of Violet's—what was she doing here? She was so much like her aunt, it would be impossible not to like her. How much should he tell her?

Oh, how he needed to tell someone the story of Violet and himself. His Violet whom he had loved so deeply.

He wanted to leave this earth feeling that his life was put in order.

He had tried to forget Violet, but with little success.

He looked up and saw Sally's concern. Before she could offer understanding, Samuel asked her a question.

"So, tell me about yourself. The only things I know are that you are Violet's niece by marriage; that she suffers one of the problems that we run into as we get older; and that you were to give me a message."

Sally began her story. "After college, I returned to Green Bay and worked in one of the banks. A bank manager job opened in Greenbriar, I applied, and here I am. I've been here since mid-March.

"I'm thankful that I grew up in a nice family that loves me. They taught me to be a good person. I have an older sister; she and her husband have a daughter. I enjoy meeting new people, but I also like spending time alone. I do love to read.

"There's a lot for people to do in this world, professionally and fun stuff. I can't do it all, but I'd like to catch as much of the rainbow as I can." Sally looked wistfully into space. "And I do want to fall hopelessly in love someday."

The last sentence was what Samuel had been searching for. Yes, this was the person to confide in.

"Aunt Violet's Alzheimer's allows her, on rare occasions, to remember small parts of the past. When you and I spoke last Saturday, I could only offer you that short message. I've never heard her, or any member of our family, speak of her being in this area."

Samuel sat staring at the lake.

"Violet was here . . . several months. A friend of her mother's lived here, and she had a daughter the same age. The girls were friends, and it was decided they would start college together at Grand Valley."

"Working in my potting shed one day, I looked up, and Violet was running her hand across the flowering ground cover. She too had ridden her bicycle." Samuel stopped speaking. He looked toward the lake again as thoughts from long ago floated to the surface. "How could Violet think I would ever forget her."

He lifted his head and looked into Sally's eyes. He became aware of a tenderness.

Her voice was soft when she inquired, "Samuel, did you and my Aunt Violet . . . have . . . an affair?" She stopped there. What right did she have to ask such a thing?

Samuel was not surprised by her question nor was he offended.

"I could never have hurt Violet in any way. I respected her. I never would have given her any reason to be troubled. Possibly our feelings were even more dangerous than what you are imagining. I tried not to feel the way I did about her. And believe me I tried not to let her know. There was an age difference of ten years or so. I admit now that it was my fault. I should have said no when she asked if she could stop by again."

The lake was calm and a fishing boat slowly trolled across their view. They watched in silence, and then Samuel went on with his story.

"Violet had ridden up the dirt road to view the lake, and then pulled to the side of the lane to admire the blue flowers. It seems like yesterday. A few times I've looked out that way and I'd swear that I see her. I've almost left the house to talk to her and welcome her back. But I know she's not there. The other day I thought you were a mirage. I was stunned when you didn't disappear."

Sally waited as Samuel remembered the past. "So simple and yet so complicated."

Samuel leaned back in his chair. Sally rose to leave because he was pale and looked exhausted.

"Wait. There's so much yet to tell, and it's time to tell it. I want someone to know the full story. Could you come back and see me again? I'm sure that Charlotte will be happy to prepare a meal."

Sally was thinking about her work schedule and her lack of social obligations. She felt compelled to do something special for this lonely stranger who had meant something to her aunt so long ago. "Yes, I'd be happy to return."

Samuel reached for her hand. "Wonderful." Then he closed his eyes, and Sally tiptoed from the room.

Stopping in the kitchen to let Charlotte know that he was resting, Sally complimented her on the lunch. Charlotte hesitated in her kitchen work. She quickly wiped her hands on a towel hanging from the refrigerator handle. She came to Sally and wrapped her arms around her in a hug.

"Thank you, you can't imagine the spark you have brought back into his life."

With that, Sally collected her bike and headed toward home. Her mind was sorting through a stack of loose thoughts.

She realized that she was peddling faster and faster. Coasting down the hill and into her yard, she felt that it had been an enlightening day.

 CHAPTER 5

Arranging spring and summer schedules around vacations, trying to accommodate as many as possible was mind boggling for Sally. That was not something she had done before.

It was exciting to hear the stories from the loan department about customers' plans and expectations. There was a lot of building and remodeling being done. The town was progressing, which was good news for the banking business.

On Thursday, she reached Charlotte to inquire as to when it might be convenient to visit Samuel again.

"He was hoping you'd call, Sally. He's been gathering pictures and mementos on a card table he had me lug up from the basement. Does Saturday tie up your weekend?"

"Not in the least. I need to go to the laundromat and run some errands. How about three o'clock?"

"Wonderful. We'll look for you mid-afternoon."

Early flowers were popping up in unexpected places. For the first time, Sally began to be interested in the spring plantings displayed near the entrance of the grocery. Maybe Samuel could give her some beginner's pointers.

Sally planned on riding her bike whenever possible. It would help keep her in shape.

Pedaling up to Samuel's gate seemed like something she'd done time and again. Samuel and Charlotte felt like family.

That made no sense as she'd only been there for one visit. She remembered something her aunt had told her. She had said that if you were extremely close to someone, their memories could be transferred and stored in that person's memory bank. Maybe she was sharing her aunt's feelings. She didn't know whether to turn and run, or stay and enjoy the strange situation.

The bank was a suitable place to work. Her life as an adult was being formed into a mold that she felt very comfortable with. Taking a deep breath, she parked her bike by the back door. The situation flowed lazily along like a brook over stones. Somewhere ahead there had to be a boulder. Sally didn't dwell on that but put a smile on her face, deciding to enjoy this day.

Before opening the screen she called, "I'm here."

Charlotte called back, "So you are. Come on in. Look who's here to greet you."

There stood Samuel in the far doorway with a welcome smile on his face. He did not seem as exhausted as he had in the past.

"The doctor gave me some energy pills so I could keep up with you two ladies. There have not been smiles in this house for so long. Charlotte and I have decided that you are a guardian angel sent to cheer us up."

Raising her hands in defense, Sally said, "Please, don't put me there. I could never live up to that."

It was decided instead that they would be the three musketeers, a jolly band of rascals.

They hungrily consumed an early supper at the kitchen table. Charlotte sent them off to the library with a wave of her hand.

Samuel and Sally hunched over the wobbly table. There were lots of snapshots of Violet as a young woman.

Samuel sat back, rested a moment and then straightened up. It was as if the curtain had been pulled aside and he was doing a one-man show.

"When Violet came by the second time, she walked into the potting shed. I continued working with the seedlings. I heard a sound of delight and turned to see what had caught her attention. It was the old scrapbook, full of shots of flowers I had grown and put in arrangements to sell. She was going to be taking some photography classes."

Samuel began to cough. Sally looked at her watch. It was past 6:00. The time had slipped by without them noticing. "Samuel, leave the table as it is. We'll continue next time."

Samuel placed his hand on hers. "Thank you." He turned and walked away, but not before Sally had seen the tears in his eyes.

Hurriedly, she went to talk to Charlotte. "We all expected too much. He has gone to bed."

Charlotte began to turn out the kitchen lights. "He takes care of himself. It's time for me to go home."

Sally placed a hand on Charlotte's shoulder. "What is it?"

"Cancer. There's not much they can do. He just waits it out. There are good times and bad. It is a demon. Today was such a good day, then he tries too hard to be his old self."

Closing the outside door, she turned to Sally. "He was just biding his time, but since your arrival he is wanting to stay as long as possible. There seems to be some things he wants to finish. It could be weeks or months. Time is so meaningful."

Charlotte looked Sally in the eye. "Will this chase you away?"

Sally gave Charlotte a soft smile. "Hey! I thought we voted to be the three muskets, or was it musketeers."

Quiet laughter filled the evening air. The two parted at the iron gate.

Sally rode home in deep thought. She had figured that was the problem. Changing her aunt Violet's or Samuel's difficulty was impossible. She just wanted to be of some use; an extra smile, anything to make a day better.

Her tire hit a rock on the bike path and she tumbled off into the grass. Just her knees were scratched, but the shock brought tears.

"Get up and be tough like me."

The boy was six or seven. He was sitting in his wheelchair, smiling at her. She pointed her finger at him. "You're right, by golly. Tough it is."

Surprisingly, the tire wasn't flat. As she rode on home, she added up all the blessings in her life. It was a lengthy list.

That evening she showered early and climbed into bed. The light was on for hours. Pondering continued to open doors but did not induce sleep. Church tomorrow, for sure. No more feeble excuses, it was time. It was past time. Possibly it would provide some answers as to how she could be of help to two special people.

Thunder rumbled and shook the house. Lightning flashed across the sky. Sally laughed. "Well, someone is listening. Maybe I'm on the right track." The light dimmed and she fell asleep.

 CHAPTER 6

Skimming through the church bulletin, Sally discovered they had a singles' group. After the service she ran into her biking friend, Susan, in the hallway. Upon inquiring for details, Susan ushered her into one of the offices. "A new recruit for you, Tom."

Before Sally could leave, Tom added her name to a list. "Just come and check us out, tonight, seven o'clock."

Sally walked into a room full of people of different ages. After a short service the question came up: Were there any takers for a bike ride south to Saugatuck for breakfast Saturday morning? Ten hands shot up, Sally's included. They'd leave the church parking lot at seven a.m., rain or shine.

Whoa, more changes. Her new existence was being molded into a pattern. It stirred excitement into the routine. A few additional ingredients and the mix would have just enough kick to offer some surprises.

When Sally checked her answering machine on Wednesday after work, there was a message from Charlotte. She sounded so upset that Sally called immediately to see what was wrong. "The doctor has insisted Samuel stay in bed for several days, and then only limited activity for a week. He says Samuel has been doing too much. The only reason Samuel has agreed to cooperate is because he is so set on talking to you about the past."

After those facts were conveyed, Sally could tell that Charlotte sounded less strained.

"Samuel says he's making mental lists so he won't forget anything." There was silence on the line, then Charlotte said, "Thank you so much for calling, Sally. Sometimes I feel like I'm stranded on an island. I'll get in touch when he can have company."

The following morning Sally called the florist. The saleslady spoke in a monotone. "Yes, ma'am, two colorful bouquets of fresh flowers sent to the old Witherspoon estate. One for a bedroom and one for the kitchen. One card saying, 'We three need to plan our strategy for continued success on our projects,' signed M3 P.S. Chin up."

The lady had kept Sally on the line making her repeat her address and charge card number several times. Apparently, having satisfied herself that it wasn't a prank, she thanked her for the order. Just before the line went dead Sally heard her say, "Sounds weird to me."

Sally couldn't stop laughing. What was the bit about the Witherspoon estate? She knew she had given the correct address.

She'd have to start her own list of questions. Also on her lunch hour she'd better present herself at the florists so they could see that she was a real person. A little kooky, but . . .

She knew how serious Samuel's situation could be, but she forced herself to treat it lightly. Among the three of them she knew that she would be the one providing strength.

It was gloomy Saturday so she packed a rain jacket in her small carrying case.

Arriving at 6:45 a.m. she pulled her car up where others were unloading their bikes. She was surprised and pleased when she heard someone call her name. It was a young man from the main downtown branch. "I didn't see you Sunday evening."

"No, but they send information around so everyone knows what's happening."

Quickly names were attached to faces. Only eight showed up. First rule she learned was when they stated a time they meant it. At seven they pulled out. It was invigorating; the path along the road was in good shape. The breakfast would last her all day. It's a wonder they didn't get kicked out. It was a grand time. The porch was cool but the laughter surrounding the two tables kept the bikers warm.

Some stayed around 'til the shops opened, but Sally had the company of two girls her age back to the church.

The service for singles on Sunday evening would be on her priority list.

She would try to think up some activities that might be interesting. She disliked eating alone, at home or at restaurants. Maybe there were others with the same hang-up.

The ratio was as she expected, more women than men. One of the other girls had told her that there were a few steadies but often there were other obligations; people come and go.

One girl on Sunday evening had given her a disgusted look. The girl next to Sally said, "Pay her no mind. She isn't happy when a new female pops up. One fewer chance for her to snag one of the men."

Sally shook her head. "It's just nice to be with a mixed group. Since I've arrived I've been busy adjusting so I've been traveling solo. I need some people to talk to. I've never been a loner."

"You'll have fun with us. We do all kinds of crazy things. Even more important is that it's a church group. So there is a serious side, and no getting involved with troubled action. To me, the part I value most is if you have a serious problem there are hands that reach out to help. I find that a great comfort."

 # CHAPTER 7

Taking her lead from Charlotte's phone call, Sally decided Charlotte needed a break in routine. She had been told that Samuel usually fixed his own breakfast, as he preferred just cereal and juice.

She hesitated but went ahead and placed a call to Charlotte's home number. Sally was relieved when it was picked up on the second ring. "It's Sally. I hope I'm not in trouble calling at this hour."

"No, I wake up around six."

"I was wondering if you'd like to meet me in town for an early breakfast tomorrow?"

"That would be lovely."

Details were arranged. If smiles could travel on phone lines, Sally was sure she could feel one coming her way.

The next morning found them seated at the local pancake house. "I had forgotten about the outside world. I've allowed myself to get in a rut. Why did I let such a thing happen? Sounds like I should be sitting in a counselor's office." Her smile had given way to an expression of loss.

"Charlotte, I asked you here to see that smile you came in with. Look up at me. You mustn't devote every minute of your day caring for others."

Sally wasn't sure Charlotte was listening. She seemed like her thoughts were somewhere else. "You are equally important. In fact, if you spend some time doing something that would please you, the cheerfulness would be passed on to Samuel."

Charlotte remained staring at her hands that lay in her lap. Then her head snapped up with a determined look and she reached across and touched one of Sally's hands. "You know, it's been a long time since anyone looked at me or cared about me." Her voice shook. "You're very kind."

"You are too good a person not to be noticed."

The restaurant was busy but neither of them realized the wait. The dark cloud had dispersed. Charlotte's eyes were beginning to sparkle. They ate what they'd ordered but couldn't have told anyone what it was.

"Oh my gosh, I've got to get to work." Sally snatched the check and hurried to the register. Charlotte was right behind her.

"If we do this again, it's my treat."

Sally whirled around and gave her a quick hug. "It's a deal."

On Thursday Sally called to see how things were going.

"I haven't had a minute. Our patient is becoming impatient. Says he's had all the fussing he can stand. Thanks a lot for the flowers. It brightened the whole scene.

"Samuel would like to ask a favor. He wonders if you would drive him somewhere. It's just a local venture."

"Sure, when does he want to go?"

"Would Saturday morning be possible?"

"That's fine, what time?"

"Ten o'clock?"

"I'll be there. What does the doctor say?"

Charlotte whispered, "He refused to ask."

Oh boy, Sally hoped this was not a bad move.

When she arrived Samuel was waiting outside. Sally called out her window, "My goodness, don't you look dashing." He wore khaki pants, a striped shirt and tie, topped off with a Michigan State cap.

Samuel climbed in the car and turned toward her with the biggest grin.

"Where would you care to be driven, Sir?"

Following his directions she pulled into a nursery. He told her to park over by the frog pond.

Samuel slowly got out from the car. Sally had just joined him and was about to ask if he'd like an arm to steady himself. There was a loud buzz, like bees were going to attack, and they were surrounded by workers. "My goodness, Samuel, you must be a favorite customer."

One of the girls laughed. "No, he's our boss, and we haven't seen him in months." Samuel's smile resembled a neon sign.

A voice shouted from the building, "What's going on out there?"

Everyone called, "Samuel's here."

Reluctantly, they cleared a path. A man, probably in his late thirties, wearing muddied gloves and wet rubber boots, marched through the crowd with a scowl on his face. When his eyes proved that the announcement was true, he stopped in his tracks. "Back to work then. He will get the opinion that I'm not capable of running his business. Off with you."

It was definitely a dismissal. The fact that he didn't call Samuel by name provoked Sally.

Everyone smiled at Samuel again. Some shrugged their shoulders, and with a quick wave they moved away.

Sally had turned to read the sign out front.

Nature's Nursery

Dedicated to keeping scenery natural

If you don't know what to do

We can help

Samuel's glow faded, and he turned to Sally. "I'd like to introduce my manager, Paul Kline. Paul, this is a friend of mine, Sally Gordon."

He didn't even nod his head in acknowledgment. The formality of the meeting painted a clear picture of a bad situation. The morning sun did not seem as warm as when they had arrived. There had been no offer to remove the dirty gloves and greet his employer with a handshake, nor to welcome Sally.

Samuel informed Paul that he wanted to show Sally the perennials and look around a bit. The man turned and walked away without a word. Sally would have liked to have made a comment like, "How's business?" but she held her tongue.

It was obvious to Samuel that Sally was extremely uncomfortable. He quickly tapped her cheek with his index finger. "Come, I refuse to let him spoil our outing. As I show you around, the employees, and longtime friends, will cheer us up."

The nursery was ablaze with color. It was organized in a way that made you want to hurry home and redo your yard. The balance of employees wiped out the earlier fiasco with hugs for Samuel and her.

Several times Sally caught a glimpse of Paul watching her. If she would look up and see him he would turn around as if busy or walk away.

She drove Samuel home in silence. As she stopped the car by the back door and turned the motor off, she felt at a loss for words.

"I'll explain the situation to you at another time. But I did so want you to see the nursery. I wanted to do it while I still had some strength." He remained seated and continued, "A change of subject. Charlotte tells me you are getting involved in some social activities. That's good for a young person like you."

He started to get out of the car then turned back. "I'd still like to tell you about Violet. Could we make a set supper date here for Wednesdays after your work?"

"Sounds good. Is this the Witherspoon estate?"

"Another time." As he walked toward the door he removed his tie and cap.

CHAPTER 8

Before leaving the bank Sally combed her hair and put on fresh lipstick. She was at the lake by six o'clock.

She was happy to hear from Charlotte that Samuel had rested after returning on Saturday, and all day Sunday.

The three of them ate supper in the kitchen again. Then Sally and Samuel went to the library.

Sally walked around the room placing a hand on some of the books. "Each one is fascinating. Different people, places, adventures, and facts. Such a wealth."

She had just pulled a chair close to Samuel's when something swooped by her head. She ducked and it made another pass. She would have hit the floor and covered her head but she glanced at Samuel and he was holding his sides and having a good laugh.

"What is it?"

"It's my friend Edgar Allan. He'll rest now in his favorite spot on the top shelf of the bookcase. It's dark up there unless the overhead lights are on. He's an educated bat. Reads all the time."

"Samuel, Samuel, do you have any more strange friends hiding about the place? Anything else that will sneak up on me?"

Samuel was still trying to control his laughter.

"Is that Edgar Allan, like in Poe?"

"The same."

"That was a raven."

"He and I talked it over. It was a mutual understanding that he was as close as I would get."

With enthusiasm Sally began rattling off information. "Born in 1809, theatrical parents. He liked the ladies, was a gambler, heavy drinker, and had paranoid delusions. Overnight fame came to him when 'The Raven' was published in 1845. Died at forty under mysterious circumstances." She caught her breath.

"For fifty-four years a man cloaked in a black hooded garment has marked Poe's birthday, on January 19th, by slinking into the small cemetery where he is buried. He places cognac and three roses on the grave, and then slips into the shadows."

Dramatically, Samuel began to recite:

> *Once upon a midnight dreary, while I pondered,*
> *weak and weary,*
> *Over many a quaint and curious volume of*
> *forgotten lore,-*
> *While I nodded, nearly napping, suddenly there*
> *came a tapping,*
> *As of some one gently rapping, rapping at my*
> *chamber door.*
> *"Tis some visitor, I muttered, tapping at*
> *my chamber door; . . ."*

Sally took the next line:

Only this, and nothing more.

"Why is it that you know all of this?"

Sally laughed. "I didn't just take business courses at college."

Samuel rose from his chair and walked toward one of the bookcases. At arm level he carefully pulled a well-worn brown book from the shelf.

"Here is a collector's item that you will want to look at." He placed it in her lap and switched the light by her chair up a notch. "I am going to leave you with this. I need to turn in. Once again I have not told you of my Violet. Next time. But I have enjoyed this evening immensely." Then Samuel left her and slipped into the shadows.

Sally ran her hands over the front cover and turned it over to look at the back. In doing so she found the edge of the pages shined like gold. Bound in the book at the back were a half-dozen lined pages. A feminine hand had written Mrs. A. Seales Douglas, Mich. March 5th 1885—.

The book was tattered. It was a library copy from the Saugatuck-Douglas district library.

Memorial Edition

A Library of Poetry and Song

William Cullen Bryant's

Family Library

It had been published in 1878, 80,000 copies.

In between two of the pages was tucked a tiny pressed flower and a small piece of notebook paper.

Mrs. SealesMrs. A. Seales

Douglas, Michigan   Douglas, Michigan

Allegan County   Allegan County

Jennir Seales Douglas

Sally could imagine the young girl who had sat in the library dreaming of her future.

She glanced at her watch. It was midnight. Carefully she returned the book to its place of honor. She then whispered, "Good night, Edgar Allan." She pulled the library door closed. Then she, too, slipped into the shadows of this house full of mystery and history. She was glad that she had parked near the door. The moon was full. The air still. A dog howled in the distance. "Goodnight, Mr. Poe, wherever you are."

 CHAPTER 9

Charlotte's last name was Barlow. Her parents had lived next door to what was now Samuel's. She had been married; her husband walked out on her. After her mother died, Charlotte returned with two teenaged sons to care for her ailing father. He had died when the boys reached adulthood. Within a year, one had moved to California and the other to Maine.

Charlotte had no idea what to do with her time. Feeling totally lost, she tried working with the flowers near the back porch, thinking that she could at least remove the extensive weeds that seemed to be thriving there.

That's where Samuel found her. They had been friends and neighbors for years. He asked if she would consider cleaning his house and cooking for him. He assured her that she would be helping him immensely, as he had allowed housekeeping chores to slide off his necessary list. The wage he offered would more than take care of her needs. So there still was a useful life ahead of her.

Sally called Samuel's to tell Charlotte that she wouldn't be able to keep her Wednesday date. The bank was having a potluck at the park. She'd not realized what a big deal it was. Much preparation went into the picnic.

It was a family thing and everyone dressed casually. Rumor was that sometimes it was difficult to recognize some of the big guys without their shiny shoes and expensive ties.

Sally apologized and said she'd see them the following Wednesday for sure.

Charlotte said, "Don't hang up. I have a surprise. After talking to you at breakfast I walked over to the library. I was looking through some travel magazines when I noticed a sign. Two of our local women travelers are going to give a class. It's called Armchair Travel. It's about some of the places I've always wanted to go.

"They also have scheduled some professors to give conversational language courses. A few cooking classes. It's Monday evenings from seven 'til nine. So, I signed up. It starts next week."

Sally was so excited. "Charlotte, that's wonderful. My gosh, you can share with me what you are learning. I've never traveled outside the states."

* * *

Sunday afternoon the singles group was planning a volleyball game at the beach. Sally was going, to watch. Then they were to stop at the church. The service would be on the lawn because of smelly attire.

Sally had difficulty finding her group because of the number of nets set up. This was something new for her. Watching was exciting.

Then the plan changed. She was playing beach volleyball. She didn't even know how. The young man next to her was doubled over laughing at her bungling. "Our group doesn't allow bystanders."

Sally felt foolish but caught on gradually. She'd have no problem sleeping this night.

But the next day at work. . . . She didn't know she had that many parts that could ache. Her fingers did not want to cooperate; and the wrists, oh, the wrists.

Mid-morning her phone rang. She had all she could do to lift the receiver. The voice was male and was laughing before he said hello. Without knowing who the voice belonged to Sally said, "Whoever you are, it's not funny."

"I'm sorry." The statement was followed by another laugh. No sincerity and Sally knew it.

"I'm Tom Brown, the mean person who pulled you from sitting on the sand into the game. I work down the street. I figure I owe you a lunch. There's a hot dog stand on the corner. Could we meet there at one o'clock?"

Sally sighed. "Will it give me some energy for this afternoon?"

"No guarantee."

"If I'm a no show, it's because I passed out on the way from extreme pain."

At one o'clock she could see him rushing past the stand. "Maybe if you lean on me."

Sally glared at him. "Do I look like the athletic type?"

Tom sat her at the small table with the red umbrella. "I'll order for you since there are no choices anyway."

Hot dogs, chips, and a root beer were gulped down, so now Sally could also have indigestion. She couldn't dislike Tom. He was too delightful.

Next thing she knew he dipped the end of his napkin in her remaining root beer and wiped the corner of her mouth. "Mustard." She tried not to laugh for fear of hurting another muscle.

"Hey, I gotta get back. By now you can tell that I'm a big spender." He grinned and was walking backward away from her. "Like to take you to a movie or something. How about tomorrow night? I'll call you."

He turned and ran into the late lunch crowd.

When Sally sat back she realized that the people at the other tables were smiling. She smiled back and shrugged her shoulders.

She chuckled all the way back to the bank and until she reached her desk. Even the people waiting in line to do their banking were looking at her.

Trying to act more dignified, she realized one thing. Laughter and a bit of foolishness helped to cure aches and pains.

CHAPTER 10

Between the two women there was a lot of talk at the supper table on Wednesday. Charlotte spoke of Province and Tuscany. The air was full of aromas of herbs and lavender. It seems that every Christmas Samuel had given her beautiful books of faraway places. This class was the answer to her desires. Neither she nor the others were planning to actually go to these picturesque places. It was exciting enough for them to be with others with the longings to be carefree travelers.

When Charlotte finished, Sally told of her date for the movies on Tuesday evening with Tom Brown.

Samuel was happy just to listen.

When they were settled in the library, Samuel began the story of him and Violet. He recalled the fact that in May Violet had come by on her bicycle. She was visiting her friend for the weekend to make plans for college. Much to her parents' disappointment, the girls decided Violet would come for the summer. To cement the deal they acquired waitress jobs, full-time starting when they graduated and part-time when college began.

It was June when Violet came by again and entered Samuel's world in the potting shed.

As time passed they took silly pictures of each other, and occasionally Samuel took some of Violet that showed proof of her beauty when she was young. Laughter surrounded their existence. The fact that she was a college student and he ten years her senior and a black man were unintentionally forgotten.

They strolled the beach whenever she was not working and had picnics on the bluff watching the sailboats. They read books and talked about everything imaginable while on the porch in the big white wicker chairs.

Violet took a fancy to the old gardener's cottage. She began to refer to it as the enchanted cottage. Every time she came by she had another addition: a welcome sign, a colorful towel. Then she began moving some lamps and fancy dishes from the big house to the cottage. She brought a hot plate she found at a garage sale, and they began having tea. Then it was treats from the bakery.

Samuel had accused her of playing house. "Nonsense," she had said. They just needed a cozy place where the winds of fall wouldn't bury them in dead leaves.

Before that they had come up with what they called a dictionary word game. Each week they'd take turns finding a word they'd never heard of and then see if the other one could guess the meaning.

One evening in October, Violet showed up with her tape recorder and a new tape she had purchased after seeing a rerun of the movie Dirty Dancing on TV. The word for Samuel to figure out was Lambada. He had no luck on that one. She said it was a Brazilian ballroom dance for couples. Violet started the tape. She reached for Samuel to pull him up from his chair so he would join her. She started demonstrating by moving her hips and asking him to move with her. He turned the tape player off, looking at her solemnly. Her face turned red and she said, "I'm sorry." Their world of happiness disintegrated. It was attacked. It crumbled. It was destroyed.

CHAPTER 11

Samuel said he had placed his hands on Violet's shoulders and was about to insist that she sit down. He needed to make her see that this was an impossible situation. He was ashamed that he had let it develop that far. He had allowed emotions to grow and bloom without trying to stop them. He loved her so much that he was in pain. He had to end something that had started out as an innocent friendship.

It was a warm enough evening that they had left the inside door open.

The headlights of a car raced into the driveway, blinding him. He put his one hand in front of his eyes to shield them. The other hand remained on Violet's shoulder. A man jumped from the driver's seat, ran to the screen door, and flung it open.

Violet screamed, "Dad!"

Grabbing her wrist, her father pulled her toward the car. "Get in the back seat with your mother."

"No, you don't understand."

He yelled at her, "I don't need to understand."

Charging back to the door, he glared at Samuel. Snarling like a wild animal he said, "If our daughter is pregnant I'll be back." Samuel could tell that the man was doing everything he could to keep from attacking him. Violet's father leaned into the screen. "What did you think you were doing?" With that he whirled around and ran to the car.

He had left the motor running. While he was turning the car around, small clods of dirt hit the screen because of the spinning tires.

Violet must have rolled a window down. As the tail lights headed toward the main road, he heard her scream, "SAMUEL."

"I remember hanging my head, not knowing how long I stood there. Finally, I slumped into a chair. What had I done? I had loved someone. I had not touched her. I didn't even act like a man and defend her or myself.

"I must have finally collapsed and slept. When I woke, the sun rays were shining through the trees. The guilt I carried outweighed my body."

He went on with his story. He was weak and listless, barely able to drag himself from one place to another. He said he knew that in order to survive he had to come out of the slump. His friends at work kept sending him home.

Many times he wondered why he hadn't been able to stand up to Violet's father. Then he realized if he had been in his place he would have acted the same. It was the following spring before he felt he could manage a natural life again. He still worked exhausting shifts at the nursery. Then he came home and fell into bed. He tried not to think of the past. His personal future didn't exist. Just getting through each day had to be enough.

"She wasn't the kind of person you forget. So often I wondered about her life, hoping it was happy. I suppose that others also thought wild things were going on here." That brought a smile to his face. "When there was no shame, no torrid love affair, just love, silent unexpressed love. I still feel it in the area of the potting shed on occasions. It swirls around me like a mist. I feel like it is alive, like I could touch it; and sometimes I feel like a hand reaches out to touch me. Then, I admit it, I cry.

"A lost love. That sounds so dramatic. I never knew for sure what she carried away with her that night. My heartbreak felt like slivers of glass. Foolish old man."

"Since she remembered you," Sally said, "even in her condition, I'd say it was not a one-sided hurt. Aunt Violet did finish college. She married a really nice man a couple of years later. They had a little girl but she died before her first birthday. Possibly that was why Aunt Violet and I were so close."

Samuel looked like he would collapse. Sally insisted he call it a night, and she left. Still Samuel acted like the telling had lifted a heavy burden from his shoulders.

When Sally arrived at her apartment, she realized she was equally tired. Maybe it would have been better to leave the story untold.

Sally remained sitting in her darkened apartment with a heavy heart. Some things can never be fixed. But Samuel had created a self-imprisonment for himself. That was the saddest part of all.

 CHAPTER 12

Sally was able to get a couple of extra days off over the Fourth of July holiday. It was good to get home to Green Bay and see the folks.

Each day she stopped by the nursing home. On July 3rd her aunt greeted her with a smile. "How's Greenbriar?" It seemed to be a general question, nothing more. Sally decided to enter the conversation as if there was a deeper meaning.

"I have met Samuel. We're becoming friends. He asks about you. He's a very interesting fellow. I go there once a week." Then she waited.

"Yes, I know. I'm so glad you have the opportunity to know him. Is he well?"

"I'm afraid not. You see, he has cancer."

"Getting old and not being well is not a good plan." She sighed, turning her head on the pillow.

Sally was afraid that might be the end of communication. Noticing a small healthy violet plant on the bedside table Sally said, "I don't see a card on this. Who is it from?"

"It was delivered yesterday, I think. It doesn't need a card or name, does it." Violet looked knowingly into Sally's eyes. Then she began to hum a song from long ago, and once more she returned to another time and place.

The following Wednesday Sally was back at Samuel's. She spoke of her aunt Violet and mentioned the little plant.

Samuel smiled. "I thought she would enjoy it. No one need know who sent it.

"The two of us spent a lot of time in the potting shed working with beginning plants." Samuel could visualize the crude sign over the door, "Leave your problems outside." He stared out the window as the grandfather clock in the corner of the library ticked away. Then he continued with his story.

Sally had to lean closer, he spoke so softly, as if he were only speaking for his own ears.

He rambled on about happiness and contentment. In reflection he spoke of the smell of herbs in the warm moist air, peeling paint, rotted wood, and watering cans. He chuckled when he mentioned Peter Rabbit.

"I do not go there anymore. It makes my soul ache. I never stepped through the door of the cottage after that night. Violet had turned it into a charming restful place. In one evening it had changed to a forbidden hideaway."

Sally felt a need to change the subject. "Who's the lady in the portrait in the dining area?"

"Oh, that's Miz Lila. You asked about the Witherspoon Estate. I should start at the beginning."

Samuel said he was born in 1933. When he was ten his parents and some other blacks moved from the South to this area. They came to work on the cruise ships docked here, and some were employed by the resort hotel on the lake. His family was hired by the Witherspoons. His father was in charge of the grounds and his mother the household. He was old enough to help his father and given small chores to do, but no one could ever find him. No one except Miz Lila.

Not long after they had settled in, Miss Witherspoon discovered him hiding behind an overstuffed chair in the library. He was almost buried in a pile of books, attempting to read. She insisted he be schooled.

Shortly after Samuel and his family's arrival the patriarch of the Witherspoon clan died. Miz Lila had been trained to take over so there was no major break in the routine. She had never married. Samuel considered her a lovely and extraordinary individual.

Before he finished high school, Samuel's parents had died also. Miz Lila put him to work in the nursery. She informed him that he would be going to college, and that he was to save his money carefully to help pay his way. His belongings were moved into the big house. That way she could keep an eye on him so that he didn't neglect his studies.

He enrolled at Michigan State. Miz Lila said he was to take business courses, anything to do with plants, and English courses. He remembered her exact words. "Your best learning tool is reading. Every day read. It will make you a learned man. It doesn't matter what you read about." He followed her advice.

Samuel's biggest regret was the Miz Witherspoon did not live to see him graduate at the top of his class. In his heart he knew how proud she would have been. Many times he had imagined her walking up to him that day. She would not have shown a great deal of emotion. She would have tilted her head back a bit so he could see her eyes, because she would have worn a large stylish hat. Then she would have claimed, "I knew you could do it, Sammy." She was the only person to call him that.

Her funeral had been the week before graduation. She had been ill for several months. Samuel had cared for her as best he could. He had come home each weekend and arranged for live-in help during the week. The lawyer did not approach him until the ceremony was over. Samuel had returned to the big house and was trying to figure out what he should do. He could not stay at the house.

The lawyer came up the walk and rang the bell. A bewildered young man answered the door. When the lawyer departed, young Samuel was sitting in the library in tears. Miz Witherspoon had left everything to him. He could not believe it.

The nursery, the house, the land. He had for a number of years thought of her as family, but he had never expected this. He knew he had to drop the feeling of being a young man just out of college. He was a man of much responsibility. She had prepared him for this without his realizing.

Samuel had remained quiet for so long that Sally thought maybe she should leave.

Finally Samuel wanted to continue. "I want to finish our evening on a lighter note. When I was a junior at college, that would have been 1953, a few of us boys went on a bit of a lark. When you mentioned that you, Charlotte, and I become the three musketeers, it reminded me of this escapade. I forgot about it until now."

Sally could tell by the sparkle in his eyes that this would be a much easier way to end the visit.

"We had heard a lot about Idlewild. It was near Ludington, one of the biggest African American resort communities in the U.S. Some black entertainers got their start there, Della Reese, Sarah Vaughn, Count Basie, to name a few. Lots to do there and numerous pretty girls. We headed that way on a Saturday and didn't go back 'til Sunday." With that he wiggled his eyebrows, laughed out loud, and slapped his thigh.

Sally had not heard him laugh like that before. "Why, Samuel, you old fox."

 CHAPTER 13

Over the next week or so Sally learned even more about Samuel's story.

The Witherspoons had started the nursery business years ago and had made a great deal of money. After Miz Witherspoon was gone, Samuel missed her terribly. It took a while for him to absorb the reality of the situation.

Once he got things going, no one could stop him. His whole being was wrapped up in the nursery. He lived in the house, but keeping that up was not a priority. He felt that houses were for families. Then Violet came into his life. After that it was another tragedy he had to deal with.

It was never with the same enthusiasm as before, but the nursery prevailed again. It was so successful he had to hire a manager. Paul entered the picture.

When Samuel interviewed him he was young, enthusiastic, businesswise, and inventive. He specialized in imaginative landscaping. Business and home owners loved him. He had been with the company for a long time.

To this day if a customer wanted his place to look great, she called

Paul. He could produce a professional look or make the property look like everything popped up on its own.

Samuel said, "He knows I have the books checked. All of a sudden he became argumentative with the help. Now, I don't know what the trouble is. He acts odd. I'm uncomfortable with it enough that I have a secondary person checking the books, on the sly. It doesn't appear that he's doing anything illegal. Unless, I never thought until now, you don't suppose he's growing something in the greenhouse that he shouldn't.

"That would tear the business apart. It has had such a good name, that would be disastrous. Still, I would find that hard to believe. Certainly one of the help would notice. They have been with Nature's Nursery for such a long time. They are so loyal." Samuel looked puzzled and annoyed.

"But if you watch any TV or read the papers, loyalty is not a word you hear often these days. Greed is a more common word."

Samuel looked beaten by his own thoughts. "I'm just not up to replacing him at this point. The business is thriving. I just hope everything is on the up and up. I don't have the energy to fight for right anymore."

When Sally spoke to Charlotte again, Charlotte told her that when the cancer struck, he thought he could fight it. But the doctor told him straight out that he wouldn't win this one.

 CHAPTER 14

By now the pattern was to go to Samuel's after work on Wednesdays. The three of them would eat supper, then Sally and Samuel would go to the library.

If Samuel was up to it and it was a balmy evening, they might stroll short distances in the yard by the lake or in Samuel's woods. He would have his arm linked with hers.

Samuel had asked if she would read to him, as his eyesight was failing. Sometimes Charlotte would join them. Samuel was the one who got to pick the readings. Sometimes he would drop off to sleep, but he always claimed he heard every word.

Sally would try to trick him by changing the printed words. Then he would raise his head and say, "No you don't."

He liked the writings of Edgar Allen Poe. There was another author he favored: Will Carleton. Farm Ballads, published in 1873. One of his favorite poems was "Over the Hill to the Poor House," and Sally liked to read it. The man's writing was melodious.

On occasions, if the weather was blustery, they might just sit and discuss problems brought to light on the TV news. It bothered Samuel that there was so much sadness. That's when Sally searched the shelves for something to brighten their spirits.

The suppers were fun because Sally would speak of happenings with the singles group. Her pal Tom Brown's activities were always worth a laugh.

Then one night in August, Charlotte hung her head and her face turned pink as she spoke of a gentleman in her travel class. That brought a bright smile to Sally and Samuel.

"Well now, tell us more."

Samuel said, "Yes, please do."

"Well, it's a mixed group and some are couples. After a few weeks I noticed that the same man had been sitting next to me. I thought it was probably circumstantial, he often uses words like that."

By this time Sally and Samuel could hardly hide their grins. Charlotte didn't seem to notice.

"Well, last evening after class, he asked me if I'd like to stop for a cup of coffee at the cafe on the corner."

When Charlotte looked up into two Cheshire cat faces, she busted out laughing.

"Oh, dear. I'm sorry. I'm being silly."

"Not silly, you're being alive."

Samuel nodded in agreement.

Charlotte started up again. "He's called T.T. He's got a bum leg. The doctor suggested he might try riding a bicycle. He could have one made special.

"I was wondering; I have a bike in my garage. Do you suppose I could ride with you a few times, Sally, before winter comes? Just in case . . . I need to be in shape."

The first Saturday in September Sally rode to Charlotte's. Charlotte insisted she come in and see where she had spent most of her years.

It was a three-bedroom ranch. Probably it could have used some repairs, but it was on a lovely lot, trim and well kept.

Charlotte hadn't thought about it before, but now she felt she needed to make excuses. "It's terribly drab." Then her voice began to sound more cheerful. "Because of your encouragement, I made myself come alive. Why can't I do the same for my surroundings?"

Sally patted her on the back. "Why not. Let's head out."

Things were going well at the bank, except when Sally interviewed new people for key positions. The main office did not agree with her suggestions. Her first choices were turned down.

September 11, mid-morning, a woman entered the bank and walked up to a teller's window. She said nothing and looked ill. The teller motioned to Sally that something was wrong.

Sally approached the woman slowly. "Would you like to sit down? Could I get you a glass of water, or call someone for you?" The woman looked into Sally's eyes.

"The Towers. I just heard it on my car radio. In New York. Airplanes ran into them. Hundreds are dead. I'm frightened."

Sally asked another teller to go to the break room and flip on the radio. She returned shortly looking pale. "Terrorists!"

The phone on Sally's desk was ringing. The teller helped the woman to a chair nearby. When Sally got to the phone, the main office informed her that they were sending over a TV to be placed in the lobby. "Our placid world in Small Town, USA, like the rest of the country, is in turmoil."

Sally called Charlotte. "Do you and Samuel have the TV on? You should turn it on. I'll stop over after work. Don't fix anything to eat. I'll pick up something on the way. At a time like this people need to be together."

Immediately after that she called her mom. Each said how relieved she was to hear the other's voice and to know that each was all right.

Then Sally pulled the staff together. "There will probably be little banking done today. Do what you can to assure people that things are as usual here. Be friendly and circulate. Keep a fresh pot of coffee going and break out more Styrofoam cups."

People came in off the street and stood mesmerized by the TV coverage. New York City was a long distance away, but emotions were as if they were next-door neighbors.

Thursday the TV was removed. Still, that's all that people talked about. Each TV station had an interview with someone who was trying to locate a family member.

By the following Monday, life had somewhat returned to normal. The incident would never be forgotten, but it was agreed that the best way to fight the perpetrators was to go back to our routines. We needed to show them that we were survivors.

The Saturday after 9/11 Tim called. "Hey, lady, I don't know about you but I want to touch base. I need the company of a good friend. Could you come to Lansing after work Friday and stay over? I'll chain myself to the sofa and you can have my bed."

"I got your letter about the fun singles group. Have you hooked up with one of those rascals?"

"Yes, I could come. No, to hookups. What about Mary, Mary, quite contrary?"

Tim laughed. "You got that right. What she was looking for was a wealthy social climber. I didn't fit the pattern at all."

"So back to old Sal, huh?"

The phone remained silent. Tim sounded serious when he spoke again. "Sally, you know better than that. I've always thought of you as a special friend. I guess I just need some reassurance after this terrorist business. I don't feel grounded. What's happening to our world?"

Sally paused a moment. "I hadn't thought of it that way. I could use some ground work myself. I haven't been sleeping well. But we must promise that we'll cheer each other up."

"It's done. See you Friday."

It was a great weekend. They did a lot of walking around the campus. Many changes had been made. The students looked like high school kids, and the two of them felt middle-aged. They took in a silly movie, ate too much snack food, and left the TV off.

Tim was putting in a lot of hours, Sally was caught up with her work. Yet each was questioning. Where do we go from here? What's next? Sally asked, "What was that song, years back? I think Peggy Lee sang it. 'Is That All There Is?'"

"I'm not sure this is doing either of us any good. We're having a pity party. This terrorist attack seems to be sidetracking us. Disturbing as it is, we need to return to our jolly selves."

She reached over and pinched his cheek. He covered her hand with his. Then he said, "Somehow it makes you feel guilty. Why them? Why not me?"

"Since we don't run the show, we had better prove we're worthy of being part of what's left."

"I think talking it through has helped. I've always felt good when I was around you."

With that Sally laughed and gently freed her hand from his. "Let's not get gushy, old friend. I need to get on the road. Thanks for the invitation. It's been fun. A rule: no correspondence unless we have positive thoughts to share."

Sally's bag was packed, and Tim carried it to her car.

She drove away, and Tim sat down on the steps. His world felt empty. It was only seconds and Sally's car was out of sight. But her presence lingered. He stared down the street.

He had a desire to run after her. He'd dealt with many things by himself over the years. Why the change? Why the feeling that it wasn't enough? Why, indeed?

In the park across the street, some college boys were shooting baskets. He went to join them. The second time one of them threw the ball to him, it thumped him in the chest and knocked the wind out of him. Tim coughed and shook his head. "You're out of the game, man. We saw the girl leave. Your mind is on the chick."

Tim grinned. "Maybe so."

 CHAPTER 15

The bikes were stored for the winter.

Sally went home for Thanksgiving because she felt required to work over Christmas, since it was her first year on the job. Violet was completely in her own world now. They didn't speak of her much because they already could feel the coming loss.

Tim had told her that he was invited to dinner by his boss and his wife.

Charlotte and Samuel were excited when Sally told them about her December plans. Charlotte hurried to Samuel's side and whispered in his ear. A wide smile became evident.

Hiding crossed fingers behind her back Charlotte asked, "Would you spend Christmas day with us?"

"Sounds like a winner to me. Would it be okay if I invited my friend Tim? I've talked about him so much it seems like you already know him. He doesn't have family."

"Oh, Samuel, a real Christmas." Turning to Sally she said, "We've always had a nice dinner but . . . We could be festive. Not overdue it, mind you, but it would be something to plan for."

"No gifts," the three agreed.

"I want to bring some things for the dinner, so we have to figure that out."

With that Charlotte bustled out toward the kitchen. She needed paper and pencil, things needed to be organized.

Samuel said, "I've never seen her so excited."

"What about her gentleman friend?"

"Seems he has children and grandchildren in town and spends the day with them."

The following day Sally put in a call to Lansing. When Tim got back to her, she told him of the invitation. There was silence. "Do you already have plans?"

From the other end came a strange comment. "Bear with me a minute, okay." It was an awkward few minutes. Sally heard him blow his nose.

Then she asked, "Do you have a cold? There are no gifts required."

"Shhh . . . I haven't been part of a true Christmas celebration since . . . I was part of . . . my own family. Basically what I have done was go to church on Christmas Eve."

"We can include that." Sally had not realized his loneliness at holiday time. Now she knew what she was dealing with. "Do you have extra days off?"

"We are working the Friday before, then not again until the 26th. I've got work to catch up on over the weekend, then I've no specific plans."

"How does this sound? You arrive here the evening of the 23rd. I have to work half a day on Christmas Eve. Hey, you can clean my apartment." No comment. "So, we'd have the afternoon, then we could attend midnight service. We would go to Samuel's for the day, then both jump back into the work routine on the day after."

"You sure?"

"I'll be expecting you."

Sally could hardly wait to tell Charlotte. This would call for special preparations.

The report was that Samuel had rested for hours, then slowly climbed to the attic and found boxes of decorations.

The singles group spent a Sunday afternoon at a cut-your-own-tree farm. They rode around on a hay wagon pulled by two big farm horses. Tom was wearing a felt jester hat his sister had made him last Christmas. He kept them all in stitches with his foolishness. Sally picked out a big tree and a tiny one for her place. She hadn't thought of having a tree, but now it was a must.

Charlotte and Sally insisted Samuel check the lights. The holiday spirit had arrived at the Witherspoon Estate.

Sally had sent the gifts off to the family. She had a short but important list to work on at the moment with no ideas. Finally everything was ready.

Tim pulled in late on Sunday. They talked for awhile, then she made up Tim's bed as they both were tired.

Tim met Sally at the door of the bank at one o'clock. They strolled the snow-covered downtown streets. The stores were still open in hopes of picking up last-minute shoppers. "They've got some decorations on sale in the window. I'm going in."

"I'll catch up with you in a few minutes. There's something I need to get." When Tim rejoined her, he was out of breath. Being afraid she might notice he said, "I was trying to catch Santa, but he hopped in his sleigh and took off." Sally was busy trying to decide which of the baubles to purchase. They ended up window shopping at a pet store.

At three o'clock they ate supper because they knew places would close early.

After they walked back to the car, they took a turn through the park and watched a freighter move into the city dock for offloading. That brought to mind how many people worked on holidays and weekends. There was a tugboat nearby lit up with strings of colored lights.

When they returned to the apartment, they watched the evening news. That was their intention anyway. They both fell asleep. Next thing they were poking each other and asking what time it was.

Tim said, "You know, we don't have to make the midnight service on my account. We both seem too tired to gain much by it."

"I know I'm pooped. Would it be all right, do you think?"

Tim ruffled her hair with his hand. "Let's call it a night."

While Sally was in the shower, Tim went down to his car and opened the trunk. Hurrying around in the apartment, he made a few changes.

Sally came out with a thick white robe on, still drying her hair. "What's the big package? No gifts, remember?"

He urged her to open it. It was a velvety soft antique ivory blanket.

"I remembered that old faded brown blanket you had at school, and I thought this one looked more like you. It says on the package that it feels great next to your skin."

Sally laughed. "I'll bet it does."

Tim excused himself, and gathered his things for the shower. Letting the hot water cascade over his body, it felt good to just stand there with his eyes closed thinking of nothing in particular. But then his mind turned to someone in particular. He turned the shower off and toweled himself dry.

With pajamas and robe on, he stepped back into her living room. She had taken the blanket from its package. Running her hand over it she remarked, "It's probably the nicest blanket I've ever had. Thank you."

She then handed him an envelope. "Tickets to the balance of State's basketball games." "Well, aren't you sweet."

"You didn't make up my bed."

"You expect me to wait on you?"

He was standing in the doorway to the kitchen. He motioned for her to join him, pointing to the top of the opening.

"When did you get that?"

"When you were deciding whether you should purchase the little snowman or the elf for your tree. The lady in the florist shop said it was her last one. I ran all the way to the car and back so you wouldn't know."

"Well, it wouldn't be right to let a sprig of mistletoe shrivel up and . . ." Sally moved toward him. Tim folded his arms around her. The kiss was not what she expected, not from an old college friend but much more meaningful than that. She leaned into him. Her response surprised both of them.

They stood back and took a long look at each other. Finally, to break the spell she said, "I bought both the elf and the snowman. They are still in the bag. Why don't we string them with yarn and each hang one on the tree?"

"If you'll get out the pillow and sheets, I'll fix my space."

"Suppose, we were to test that blanket to see if the advertising is correct."

"This isn't just being nice to a poor lonely man over the holidays, is it?"

"That's an insult to both of us. I thought you said you knew me."

"Maybe not as well as I should."

They snuggled under the blanket on the sofa, each commenting on how soft and warm it was. Sally, then, hopped up and went to the linen closet for the bedding.

Christmas morning it was cold and the sun made the snow sparkle. Tim looked at the clock on the end table. They'd slept in. He knocked on Sally's door. She mumbled. He went in and touched her on the shoulder.

"So, dear heart, how did the blanket feel next to your skin?"

"Great. What time is it?"

When Tim told her, she moaned. "Gotta get up and at 'em. It's Christmas Day."

Turning toward him, she looked into his eyes for a long time. Then she winked and grinned. Wrapping the blanket around her, she ran toward the bathroom, reaching for clothes on the way. He tried pulling at the blanket but she was too fast. When she came out, she was dressed all but shoes.

Tim came out complaining about the steam bath she'd left behind. "How's a man supposed to shave?"

They had cereal and coffee because of the big dinner coming up. After packing the dishes in the car, they sang "Over the River and Through the Woods" all the way to Samuel's.

Sally got out and was waiting for Tim to pass her some of the things that had to be carried in. He walked to her side of the car and surprised her with a big kiss instead. "If you don't stop that . . . well, a girl like me is likely to . . . misunderstand."

Tim put his face close to hers. "My dear, you are not misunderstanding anything."

Samuel knew the minute they hit the house. Laughter, what a wonderful sound. He had been looking out the window when they pulled up. He wanted to meet this young man.

The smell of turkey and dressing carried outside, and when they opened the door they both took a deep breath. Sally put her Jell-o salad in the refrigerator and the rest of the things on the kitchen table. She then handed Charlotte her gift.

When Charlotte saw what it was she said, "I won't dare wear it, white cotton with eyelet and lace. It's so lovely."

"You must. After the gravy and stuff is cleared, you can put it on. It's washable."

She had introduced Tim. Charlotte wrapped a towel around his waist and put him right to work.

Charlotte stepped into the pantry. "I have something for you, too."

Sally unwrapped it. "A cookbook. Perfect. I need this."

"I got one with lots of pictures 'cause you said you liked pictures."

Sally hurried into the library and gave Samuel a kiss on the cheek, handing him his gift. She'd gone to the used book store and purchased two first editions. "Wonderful. What a dear you are!"

There was a wrapped box on a table by his chair. He handed it to Sally. It was a music box. When Sally lifted the lid it played, "The Hills Are Alive with the Sound of Music." It was lined with purple velvet. She closed the lid. "Thank you, Samuel." He patted her hand. She kissed him on the cheek again and hurried from the room. She didn't want him to see her tears.

Tim was brought in from his kitchen duties so the two men could meet. Samuel hoped they would have a few minutes alone before the day was over. Tim had wiped his hands before entering the library. Samuel was impressed with the young man's firm handshake.

Before Sally scooted out to the kitchen to help, Samuel spoke to her again. "A boy came by the other day selling magazine subscriptions for his school. I ordered some for you. That's part of your gift also. I have no idea when they will start arriving. Always hate to turn the lads down. You know how it is."

When they were finished with the meal, Samuel spoke, "A fire going in the library, a Christmas tree, friends, and a delicious traditional holiday dinner, what more could a man ask for?" Goblets with ice water were raised and a rousing, "Hear! Hear!" was heard around the dining room table.

Sally had insisted that Charlotte show off her apron, so she was parading around the table.

Sally heard a tap on the back door. Puzzled as to who it could be, she opened the door a crack. "Hello."

The gentleman removed his hat. "And a hello to you, Miss."

Sally's mouth opened in surprise. "Might you be who I think you are?"

He smiled and put his hat back on.

"I have a package for Miss Barlow. You see, Samuel reached me the other day and said he thought it would be a fine thing if I were to show up for dessert."

"Come in. Wait here."

Sally marched back into the dining room. "Charlotte, you have not put out enough dessert plates."

"Surely I have."

"There is a man at the back door claiming he is hungry. It seems wrong to turn him away."

"I don't believe in Santa Claus."

"Maybe you should."

Charlotte's face turned crimson and she rushed out. Immediately the door swung open again. "This is my friend from class."

Three voices in unison said, "Welcome, friend from class."

After everything was cleared and dessert and coffee were served. Samuel said, "I hate to put a damper on things but I am happily tired and need to leave you all. A memorable day for sure." They all agreed.

Sally and Tim knew that Charlotte would be escorted home, so they left.

"What a day."

"That it was."

Upon reaching the apartment Sally asked, "Would you like me to make up the sofa?"

"I'll leave that up to you."

"Maybe we should check that blanket again. I wonder if it has a warranty."

CHAPTER 16

The sun broke on the year 2002. The stores looked bare when all the red and green decorations were stored for another year. It seemed good, almost like a cleansing, not so much clutter.

Wednesday nights at Samuel's were postponed until the second week. He was getting weaker. The holiday enthusiasm had sapped his energy.

The following Wednesday Sally's dad called with the news that Aunt Violet was slipping fast. Sally left a message on Samuel's answering machine saying only that she had to be away. She made arrangements at the bank and for her flight home.

Sally did not arrive in time to say good-bye.

There was sadness, but it was as it should be; Violet had not been responsive for several months.

As soon as she got back to Greenbriar Sally dropped her bags in the apartment and drove out to the old estate. She had been unable to speak to Charlotte before leaving.

She knocked, then entered without hesitating. After bringing Charlotte up to date, she went to the library to speak to Samuel. The fireplace was crackling. He looked so peaceful in his chair, it was a shame to wake him.

Then she realized, there was no need. Returning to the kitchen Sally stood just inside the door. When Charlotte looked up, she knew by Sally's face that Samuel was gone. They hugged each other tight for several minutes, overcome with grief.

They sat at the table getting their wits together. Arrangements had previously been made, but they needed to get things rolling. First they called 911.

At times like this, time seems to stand still. All of a sudden Sally raised her head and smiled. "Maybe he knew about Violet. Possibly, they are together now."

"We knew it would come. Maybe our prayers kept him here too long."

⊠ CHAPTER 17

Sally immersed herself in her work. She knew she should call Charlotte, but her mind was so shut down that she didn't make the effort.

On Friday she received a phone call from the lawyer's office. She had forgotten that a man had handed her a business card at the cemetery. It was probably still in her coat pocket.

Lloyd Webster's secretary was beginning to explain the call when Mr. Webster took over. "Miss Gordon, I wouldn't be pushing you, but one of the people in Samuel's will wants to get things moving."

Sally couldn't figure out why he should be calling her about this.

"It's possible that you haven't received your notification yet, because I mailed them out just yesterday, but you are mentioned in the will. We cannot proceed without your presence. Would you be available Saturday at ten."

"Yes, certainly. Where is your office?"

"The second floor in the Carnegie Building."

Why would her name be mentioned in Samuel's will?

At closing time, as Sally walked to her car in the parking lot she stopped. Suppose that Samuel had bequeathed to her a couple of their favorite reading books. What an exciting thought.

Saturday, January 26th, Sally arrived at the lawyer's office fifteen minutes early. Charlotte was there ahead of her. Three chairs set up across from the lawyer's desk.

Sally apologized for not calling. "I can't seem to function properly."

"I feel the same. No excuse needed."

Paul came through the door. Looking at Sally he asked the lawyer, "What's she doing here?"

"Her name is listed in the will." Paul looked disgusted.

So, the reading of Samuel's will began.

"Charlotte Barlow is to receive $100,000.00, which must be used to travel to new places."

Charlotte sat back, then turned to Sally with tears in her eyes. Sally squeezed her hand.

"Paul Kline is legal owner of Nature's Nursery." For some reason Paul became fidgety.

Mr. Webster paused, then continued. "Sally Gordon is to receive the balance of the estate. The land, the house, and all monies from investments."

Sally couldn't catch her breath. She was in shock. She could not have heard right. The blood drained from her face.

Paul jumped to his feet, turning the chair over on its side. His eyes were afire like red hot coals. He started yelling. Putting his face even with Sally's, he spit out his next words. "Who are you?"

"You took up all of his time. He confided in you, never in me. I worked for him for years. I should have had it all. What did you do out there where no one could see you? Is this a payback for services rendered?" The smile on Paul's face was vicious.

Both Sally and Charlotte gasped. Mr. Webster was about to ask him to leave but decided to finish this once and for all.

Sally felt sick. She was shaking.

"Mr. Kline, the nursery is worth a substantial amount of money, and it's yours. It has a great future. It should more than provide you with a fine living."

Paul glared at him. "I'll bet you got your fingers in the pot, too. All lawyers are crooks. We'll see about this." With that he charged out of the room, slamming the door and breaking the old fashioned glass in its upper portion to shreds.

Sally was so shaken she was sobbing, never having been in a stormy situation like the scene that had just erupted. She was so confused, she needed some answers. "Mr. Webster, is something wrong here? I don't know anything about legal matters. Has there been a mistake? I don't want to get in trouble with the law."

"No, Sally. This will was completed in November. There is no mistake. Samuel knew exactly what he wanted to do. He left Paul a legacy that he may not have deserved. I don't know what his problem is. Hopefully, after he thinks it over and realizes what he has been given, he will be a happy man."

Then rising from his seat he said, "Charlotte, I'm going to have my secretary see you to your car. I need to talk about some details with Sally."

When he turned back, Sally was bent over, her elbows on her knees, resting her head on her hands.

Lloyd Webster gave her a few minutes. He set the chair upright. "Suppose I should have replaced that antique glass a long time ago." He returned to his desk and waited.

Sally raised her head. "Is that what people thought of me? When you called I thought maybe Samuel left me a couple of our favorite books.

Instead he left me the whole library. The books alone must be worth a small fortune. I can see why Paul might feel angry. It should be referred to as the Mansfield Memorial Library. Why did he do this, Mr. Webster?"

"You better call me Lloyd. For a while we are going to spend quite a bit of time together. You are a very wealthy young woman, whether you realize it or not. There are stipulations. The main one being that you cannot sell the property. There are lots of details we need to talk over. Why don't you go home and run it around in your head a bit. You will have many questions. You call when you're ready and we'll get down to business."

CHAPTER 18

Sally had stepped on the first step of her porch before realizing that she had walked home, leaving her car in the lot by the lawyer's office. Turning around, she headed the few blocks back to pick it up. Tacking words on about how she felt was easy: confused, frightened, and exhausted.

This couldn't be real. Could she handle this? She didn't even know all the facts yet.

After arriving home for the second time, she filled her bathtub with hot water. As she slowly climbed in, the water forced her to relax. Within minutes she felt like nodding off. Not wanting to be an item on the front page—WEALTHY YOUNG WOMAN FOUND NAKED IN TUB DIED OF NATURAL CAUSES—she climbed out.

She put on her pajamas and robe. After rinsing the tub, she stepped into the living room. The sofa looked inviting. She'd just lie down for a minute. It was still light out when she drifted off.

The ringing of the phone pulled her from a deep sleep. It was dark outside. "Hullo."

"Is that you, Sal?"

She was still groggy. "Who's this?"

"Tim."

"Oh, Tim. Oh, Tim! I wish you lived closer, then you could come over and I could talk to you. So much has happened. You won't believe it. I can't discuss it over the phone. I'm mixed up. I must talk to you."

"Are you okay?"

"That's a good question. I must be. If I was a person of magic, I'd twitch my nose and you'd be sitting here next to me."

"That can be arranged."

"I don't have any idea what time it is, but it's dark outside."

"I don't know what's going on but I aim to find out. I'm going to toss a few things in a duffle bag and I'll be there in no time."

"I'll leave the porch light and hall light on and the door unlocked. Drive carefully."

When Tim arrived, Sally was curled up on the sofa sound asleep. He placed his hand on her shoulder. She jumped so quickly they butted heads.

"Oh, Tim." She wrapped her arms around him and placed her head on his shoulder.

"The greeting was worth the drive. Are you going to tell me what this is all about?"

"You want any coffee or pop?"

"No, I want you to tell me what has upset you."

They sat side by side on the sofa. An hour or two later Tim took a deep breath and sat back against the cushion. "No wonder you are so bewildered."

Once again Sally looked like she was going to fall asleep where she sat.

"Come on, I'm tucking you in bed." He did just that, and she was out like a light.

He stepped into the bathroom and stripped down to his shorts and T-shirt.

He went in to check on her and remained there for a long time watching her sleep. Looking around he found that old blanket from school folded up on a footstool.

Quietly, he lay down beside her, on top of the covers, and pulled the brown blanket around him. He was unable to sleep. Her life was chugging along at top speed while his was standing still. This was one complication he had never dreamed of. As time went on, wouldn't their newfound feelings disappear? Her whole life would change. Eventually he slept.

Sally smelled coffee, cinnamon toast, and bacon. Stretching, she called out, "What time is it, Chef?"

"Eleven o'clock."

"Can't be, I don't sleep that late."

When she came to the kitchen door, Tim smiled and pointed toward the clock with the spatula he was using for the eggs.

"I feel some better. Did you sleep? I was a poor hostess."

"I got a few winks. Saying that you are poor is a falsehood."

"Stop that, you know what I mean." Sally frowned. "Are you not going to like me anymore because of this silly business?"

"To be perfectly honest, I figure it might be the other way around. Let's eat."

Sally sat still, with her frown still in place and pouting. Her appetite was gone. "Maybe I could refuse to accept the gift and give it to the city instead."

"Come on, eat your eggs before they get cold. If Samuel had wanted to give it to the city, he would have done that. As you said, there are a lot of details that you don't even know about yet. Buck up, girl, we'll still be pals."

Sally felt so dejected. But . . .

Tim stood to put his plate and silver in the sink. As he walked by her, he gave her a peck on the cheek. Sally didn't know whether to cry or laugh. Their relationship had changed, and she liked it this new way.

"If you don't eat that fine breakfast I fixed you, I won't reveal my thoughts on what you told me last night."

Tim pulled his chair next to hers. "I feel that your problem is that you are thinking of the whole picture, which is overwhelming. Because of that you are afraid. You aren't even sure what is expected of you at this point. Here's the punch line: you are avoiding the challenge with feeble excuses. Just do one thing at a time. I'm sure that Samuel did not expect you to do whatever by the end of this month."

Sally rose from the table, stood by Tim, and put her cheek next to his. "You are a wonderful friend. I don't know how I would survive without you."

Tim put his hand up to hold her face where she had placed it but was afraid to respond. At the moment his heart was jumping the tracks as Sally's train went speeding by.

After doing the dishes, they bundled up and drove out to the Witherspoon Estate. Sally admitted it was the same as when Tim had come to visit the first time. Her escort service, once again, was not familiar with the lay of the land.

They spent the balance of the afternoon investigating outbuildings. When they stepped into the cottage, Sally felt like her heart would break. Samuel had told the truth. He had never stepped through the door again.

Rats had been very pleased to use furniture stuffing for nests. The tape recorder Violet had brought was still plugged in. Some small animal had worked the tape out from the machine and unwound it. There were two cups with dried, crusted tea in the bottom. A china tea pot had been knocked to the floor and broken. A lamp was tipped over, its shade had disintegrated with time. A welcome sign was tilting, the colors had faded. China plates were covered with mice droppings. Some fancy linens were in shreds. Sally's intake of breath had Tim asking, "What?"

Sally pointed. Next to one of the chairs sat a pair of ladies shoes. They were covered with mold.

Tim turned her toward the door. "Let's get out of here."

"It's like prying open an old rusty trunk and feeling sorry about what you discovered."

"What do you say we call it quits for today? Let's go somewhere where it's warm and cozy and get something to eat. Somewhere where we can hear voices of the present and not the past."

Tim took her hand, and they walked back to the car. He pulled up to a little place overlooking the lake. Sally was about to open the door when Tim asked her to sit a few minutes before going in.

"Have you been in the house yet?" Sally shook her head no. "I'd suggest you don't prowl around by yourself. The nursery manager sounds strange to me. I want to talk about this out here. When you enter the restaurant, I want your mind to be clear of all this.

"Try to relax and enjoy yourself. What you have been offered is a rare and wonderful opportunity. I can see that you will have some tough times getting things to the point where you can put a positive handle on anything."

A decision was made to only do incidental things until the weather improved. Tim also brought up the idea that it might be wise to inform the police about her plans. Maybe they would be willing to cruise up through there on occasion.

There was a fireplace inside the restaurant and it prompted just the feeling they were looking for.

At the apartment, Sally absentmindedly made up the sofa for Tim.

Early in the morning when he left, he stood directly in front of her and placed his hand on her cheek. Sally leaned into it. "Thanks so much for driving over."

"Take care of yourself, girl. If you need me, call, okay."

Tim's ride home was miserable. He doubted that she would be needing him for much. He had perked up to cheer her but in the pit of his stomach, he had the awful feeling that this was the beginning of the end. He pulled into a highway rest area to use the men's room. From then until he went home from work that day, he moved like a zombie.

CHAPTER 19

When Sally got home from work on Friday, the 1st of February, her mail was stacked on the hall stairs. What a pile. She rushed up to take care of her coat and put her purse in its spot by the telephone. Wrestling the bundle up the stairs, she was relieved when she got to the kitchen table. Curiosity was at its peak. Magazines. Samuel's Christmas gift. Most were pertaining to restoring houses, how to beautify with color, potting sheds are in, and how to start a bed-and-breakfast. She shook her head. What a sneak he was.

She'd made an appointment with Lloyd Webster for the following day at ten. When she arrived he was on the phone. He motioned for her to come into the inner office and have a seat.

When he hung up the phone, he looked at her and smiled. "You look in better shape today."

"Thanks. It's a cover-up. My brain hasn't yet found a file drawer where I can store this shocking information. I still haven't told my folks. I wanted to have a better understanding myself first. It's scary. Help me out, Mr. Webster. . . ."

"Lloyd."

"I just can't. Could I please call you Mr. Webster?"

To make Sally more comfortable he said, "When my mother was angry with me, she'd put on a stern look and say, 'WEBSTER.'"

"I'll remember that."

The lawyer spoke a few minutes about his and Samuel's friendship over the years. They'd spent many hours fishing, never talked much. Their jobs required enough talking. The silent companionship was worth more than words.

One of the things he mentioned was Samuel's difficulty when he wanted to expand the nursery. "He went to the bank where you now work. They gave him a run-around and finally refused the loan. It was a well-established business. Samuel owed no one a penny. He was furious.

"So, he did all his banking in a town south of here. They were pleased to have his business. Because of that it will be a little inconvenient for you. That's who I was talking to. They will be more than happy to sit down with you and go over his, and now your, accounts. You will need to go down and sign some paperwork. I'll need to accompany you because of getting into the safety deposit box. They are very accommodating. They should be."

In her mind, Sally tacked the name Webster on to the fine elderly gentleman.

He reached for a large folder that he'd placed on the corner of his desk. Opening it he asked Sally to move her chair so she could see, in black and white, what he was talking about.

"The property itself is worth millions because of where it is." He spoke of the buildings and how rundown the house was. "Do you know why he left it to you?"

"I barely knew him, only a few months really. We bonded so quickly that it seemed more like years."

"Part of it was in memory of your aunt. He said if he had married and had a daughter he would have wanted her to be like you."

Webster repeated the fact that it could not be sold, outright. Maybe in later years. Samuel felt that Sally had an imagination and could make something special out of it.

"He said you could make it into a family home or come up with something unique. That you could take your time and that you were to enjoy doing it."

"I don't have any money to change it back to its original splendor."

"Yes, you do. Samuel never spent money on vacations or fancy cars or frivolities. He seemed happy doing everyday things. His work in the nursery pleased him. To have what was necessary for a decent existence was all he needed."

Webster stressed the fact that Samuel kept the nursery business completely separate, financially.

Sally said, "I wish he could have had a much happier and complete life after my aunt."

"The problem with people like us is that we want to live our own lives and other people's also. We think if they don't do what we think is the right thing that they can't be happy. It's possible that Samuel was comfortable with the life he chose. He did not seem to lack satisfaction. He appeared to be content."

Sally looked a bit sheepish. "You are a wise man."

She looked at the figure where Webster was holding his finger. Leaning back in her chair, she shook her head in shock. "That's an unbelievable sum of money, and that statement comes from a person who works in the banking business."

"If you handle things wisely, you will be able to rebuild and restore anything on the land to your specifications. You would never have to work for someone else another day.

"If instead you are planning on wild parties and trips to foreign ports, well . . ."

Sally didn't hear Webster's last comment. Putting her fingers of her right hand to cover her mouth, she sat very still. "Incredible, it will be the undertaking of the century. So, you think I should plunge into this, learning as I go."

"I will be available for any legal advice."

"What is your fee?"

"There may be none. It will depend if you get yourself in some kind of trouble."

"Speaking of trouble, my friend Tim suggested that I might want to speak to the police because of Paul being so livid when he was in your office. Also with there being no one living out there, there might be a problem of breaking in and looting."

"Tim?"

"He's been a special friend since college."

"I'm sorry to hesitate, sometimes in a case like this friends pop up that you didn't know you had. I'm not trying to make you uneasy, but your position in life has changed drastically.

"There will be times when you must be wary. When you need to run a check on a person or business. Don't hesitate to ask for help. Be sharp, be smart. Don't neglect the old adage, 'If things sound too good, they most likely are.' It might be an excellent idea to speak to the police. Even if they can't do an occasional drive-through, they will be aware of the situation if a problem arises."

Sally returned to the apartment. She had been going to write a long letter to her folks and spill out the whole surprise. She was sitting with paper and pen in hand. No, it was impossible.

"Hello, Mom."

It just didn't sound like their Sally. "What is it, honey? What's wrong? Wait, I want Dad on the other line."

"Nothing's wrong. In fact, it's so right that it's scaring me."

"A boyfriend, a husband, a baby?" her dad asked.

Sally laughed. "Oh, Dad, stop it. But thanks for making me laugh. It felt good. I needed it."

"I told you that Samuel died right after Aunt Violet. A few days after, a lawyer called me to say that I was mentioned in the will. I was excited because I thought maybe he had left me a couple of the books that meant so much to him." Sally began to cry. "I'm sorry, this is hard. He left the nursery business to his manager, a good sum of money to Charlotte."

She was crying again. Her dad prompted, "Spit it out, girl. Then you'll feel better. Whatever it is you know we love you."

"He left me . . . the mansion, the property, and the balance of the estate. Which happens to be numerous investments amounting to a large sum of money."

The line was dead.

"Mom, Dad?"

It was her Dad who broke the silence. "You thought you were surprised. We are sitting here in complete shock."

"I need you, I need to see you. I need my mom and dad for support. I need you to hold me and say, 'You can handle this, Sally. This is big, big, but you can do it.'"

"We can fly in next weekend. I've got to get your mom a glass of water before she passes out. I'll call you later with times."

Although she was totally wrung out, Sally drove to Charlotte's. She wanted to approach her about helping with the beginning phase of this project.

When Charlotte answered Sally's knock, she took hold of her arm and said, "Get in here, Miss. You look pale. Come sit down, I'm going to make you some tea."

"I just got off the phone with my parents. I imagine they look the same as I do about now. I wanted to speak with Mr. Webster again before giving them a call. They will fly up next weekend. I need a little parental backup. Someone who will honestly tell me that this whole thing is okay. I feel somewhat like a thief."

Sally explained why she had driven out.

Charlotte admitted that she was afraid that she wouldn't be asked. "I have to think awhile before taking off on any big jaunt. I'd like to go to each of my son's homes for a couple of days and personally tell them what has taken place."

She told Sally that she had never been on the second floor of the mansion. "Another thing, I made the statement that I loved Samuel, and I did. But I now realize that the feelings were not how a woman loves a man. They were strong, but more like a best friend or a brother. We were very close. He was the kindest person I had ever known."

She assured Sally that whenever she needed help to let her know. She warned her about wearing anything other than grubby clothes, that no matter what they tackled, they would be filthy within the first ten minutes.

Sally said, "I'll pay you for your time."

Charlotte shook her index finger at Sally. "Pay me! Shame on you for allowing such a thought to cross your mind. Believe me it will be a major task. You'd be surprised how little I know about the big house. It will be like a treasure hunt. Count me in."

The following day Sally put on some old boots and went out to the estate. It was a tad warmer so the snow was sloppy. She didn't tarry long nor enter the house. Even being there did not fully convince her that it was hers.

Sally often caught herself staring out the windows as she sat at her desk at the bank. To try and break the spell, she'd make the rounds talking to the staff. This had to stop. She must give her full attention to her job.

That Friday, February 8th, was the opening ceremony of the 2002 Winter Olympic Games. She'd always followed them closely. Sally made herself comfortable on the sofa. Let the games begin. At eleven she was still sitting in the same spot. There was one problem. She had not seen the U.S. teams march in, nor any of the other countries.

Her attention span was nonexistent. Samuel, what have you done to me? Admit it, ninny, it's not his fault. You're the one who's responsible. Stuff yourself in a canning jar, shake yourself up, and when you pour yourself out, be credible.

Sally had to laugh at herself.

When her folks walked into the waiting area at the airport, Sally rushed up to them. The three clung together for several minutes. Their strengths were flowing into her body; she could feel it. It gave her the lift she needed.

After dropping their luggage at the apartment, Sally's dad drove her car and she directed him to the lake. It was the first time she had entered the house. She wanted to show them the library. Besides Samuel and Charlotte, she had talked about this room.

The three of them sat quietly, allowing the aura of Lake Michigan to lull their senses. Looking at each other, they smiled and were returned to reality. The world had not paused because of what had taken place. Sally had been chosen to regroup, to make unexpected changes, to blossom and thrive. After all, was this not a place that had been nourished by growing living things.

Sally looked at her folks. "I feel better already. Your coming has meant so much. I had been floating through the air, like a balloon with no purpose, and my air was slowly seeping out.

"Let's stop next door. I want you to meet Charlotte."

When her parents left on Sunday, they promised periodic visits to see the progress.

Monday after work, Sally stopped by the police station to talk to an officer. He promised that, if they were not busy and were out that way, they'd check around.

He also gave her another good idea: when she began rebuilding and there was big equipment on the property, it might be wise to hire an agency that could check things out on a regular basis.

Chapter 20

In mid-February, Sally was summoned to the home office of the bank. The head man wished to speak to her. Since it was only a few short blocks she decided to walk. She hoped she was not in trouble because of having to be absent for her aunt's and Samuel's funerals. They had seemed very understanding when she'd requested the time.

Upon entering the office area, Sally smiled at the receptionist and gave her name.

She was seated and looking through a magazine when she realized that the door to the inner office was open just a crack. The president of the bank was not alone. She could hear another voice. It was guttural sounding and loud. Sally had a feeling that it wasn't a client. She had no right to listen in on their conversation.

"She's always wanting to promote or hire someone, shall we say, from another ethnic group. We have to have a handful throughout the system but she gets carried away. Always claiming that they are the most suitable for the position."

The second person spoke. "I hope she didn't think Little Black Sambo was going to leave her anything. I wonder what they did out there at the estate. Rumors were that she was a regular . . . visitor."

They got a good laugh out of that one.

There was that comment again. Sally was careful not to change her facial expression or her body language.

"He wouldn't have had anything to leave her unless it was some kind of . . . well, you know."

More laughter.

Sally had to think fast. No matter what her reason for being here, it had just changed.

The intercom buzzed. The secretary said, "The president will see you now."

Sally stood, hoping she looked casual and confident. She put a smile on her face as she entered the door.

Quickly she checked out the second man. He wore a rumpled out-of-season suit that didn't cover up the fact that he should have purchased a larger size. Run down, unpolished shoes matched his attire. Puffy cheeks and a smile gave away the fact that he was about to witness a young lady get a verbal beating.

There would be no obvious injuries. There was no introduction of the man whose eyes gave away his eagerness to get his jollies by watching what was to take place.

By this time, Sally could hardly contain herself. Her eyes had become the eyes of a wild cat who is ready to pounce. A small but dangerous smile had appeared on her lips. Sally waited.

The president said, "Miss Gordon, we have been satisfied with your work up to now, but . . ."

Sally interrupted. "I'm glad you called me in today. I'd like to orally hand in my resignation."

The shock on the two faces would have looked great enlarged and framed and hung above a fireplace or in a public bathroom.

"I can give you a two-week notice, stay until you get a replacement, or clean out my desk today. The staff there can handle things just fine. There are several people on staff who could fill the position."

The two were still sitting there stupefied. Sally cleared her throat. With that, they blinked their eyes.

It reminded Sally of the row of stuffed cotton cats at the county fair. You throw balls at them and if you hit one and it topples over backward you get a prize. These two weren't the prize, that's for sure.

All Sally could think of was, Don't laugh, don't you dare laugh.

The president was trying to regain his composure. "Have you accepted a job somewhere else? For higher wages?"

What an incredible thought. The president was well aware that such questions were out of order.

"Yes, I'll be in charge of a project that will take me several years to complete. About cleaning out my office?"

Accompanying a vacant look, he mumbled, "Today will be fine."

The other man was still sitting there with a blank look on his face. Both appeared deflated and dysfunctional.

Sally left them, hoping recovery would be painful. Closing the door behind her, she rested against it for a moment with her head down.

She noticed the secretary flick off the intercom. "You pulled off quite a coup in there."

Sally glanced at the woman's nameplate. Lois Zwir. "How long have you worked here, Lois?"

"Too long."

Sally quickly wrote her home phone number on a tablet she carried in her purse. "Call me sometime if you're interested in making a change."

What kind of hold did that man have on the bank president? It had to be something powerful. The association was an odd one. Maybe they had hired her because she wasn't a local and they felt she could be manipulated. Strange.

Now she understood Samuel's comment to the funeral director; he didn't want people walking over his grave.

In comparison, Samuel had humble dignity. He may have been a bit eccentric, but Sally found his respectability unquestionable. However, she did have to admit, there was a lot she didn't know. After all she had only been here a short time.

Sally hurriedly left the building. Upon returning to her desk she resumed what she had been doing prior to the main bout. She was proud of herself. She declared herself the winner. After the employees had left, she gathered her few personal belongings. Leaving her key on the desk, she smiled, and walked out. Yes sir, this would have been a situation Poe would have found intriguing.

That evening at seven, Sally's phone rang. "Hi, this is Lois Zwir. I'd like to talk to you."

"At this point I'd rather we not be seen together in town. If you are not interested in what I'm considering, I don't want to jeopardize the job you have."

"Saturday my daughter has horseback riding lessons at a ranch west of town. I can take her and pick her up, of course, but have to make myself scarce for that hour or so. I take a thermos of hot chocolate and read in the car. Would that work for you?"

"Sounds good." The time was set and directions given.

The following morning Sally climbed into the cab of Lois's pickup. After a cup of cocoa with marshmallows Sally shared just the basics.

"Samuel Mansfield left me the lake property in his will. At this point I don't want to discuss details. I would rather that you did not spread this information around the community. It will all come out soon enough. I need an assistant, a secretary, a something. I need books and records set up. I can't do it all. It's got to be done in detail, all expenses, all honest and legal. There's money to work with. I am going to restore the estate. It scares me to say it.

"I can't tell you what all the job will entail. I can't offer you benefits but I will match the salary you are getting now, maybe with an increase later. I've got a lot more questions than answers. I'm new at this. I have hired people before but not when I was totally in charge. Tell me about yourself."

Lois said, "Slow down before you explode. Open your window and take a deep breath. I don't get benefits at the bank. They have me at thirty hours to make sure of that. My husband is an accountant and runs his own business out of an office in our house. He would be more than happy to help us if we run into a snag."

At this point, Lois rolled her window down a little to let in some fresh air. "I'm getting as excited as you are. We have just the one child, one dog, one cat.

"I worked part-time so we had some extra money to do fun things. Because of our setup, my husband has insurances and those kinds of things covered."

"Oh my gosh. I'm glad you mentioned that. I need to immediately set up some programs for myself. Maybe he could steer me toward the best way to do that. I have to be covered for medical purposes and others. Also I'd feel better with a well-thought-out retirement plan."

They sat for a few minutes, letting the information soak in.

"At the beginning I need a part-time investigator to work with me. Someone to compile the endless list of things to be done."

"Sounds like an adventure and a half. Well?"

"Well?"

Two voices carried out into the cold morning air. "Let's do it."

"I'll give a two-week notice and just tell the bank that I want to spend more time with my family."

"Don't contact me until a week or so after you've been home. That will give you a break and me a chance to get my thoughts organized better.

"I'll look forward to hearing from you in about three weeks, then we'll work out some kind of a schedule that suits each of us. So that no one wonders why two women are meeting here I'm going to approach the instructor about some possible lessons in the future. I'm supposing that she also deals with adults. Is it okay if I use you as a reference?"

On the way to the barn Sally passed Lois's daughter. "How'd it go today?"

"Really well, thanks."

Sally introduced herself to the teacher and mentioned Lois's name. She questioned the teacher about a brochure and said it was something she might consider down the road apiece.

As Sally drove home she thought of how circumstances change. Before she had spoken the words aloud, she hadn't thought about what a huge, huge job lay ahead. It would be complicated. She would need a couple of, at least part-time employees. It would be a learn-on-the-job proposition.

The bank president and his friend had registered so far below a fine gentleman like Samuel. What a pity that they hadn't known him.

No formal employment now, so she could postpone getting her act together no longer.

The next several weeks the lights from Sally's apartment were on into the night. Sometimes she fell asleep with her head down on the kitchen table.

One night at eleven, her phone rang and startled her. "Hello."

"Just wondering if you were okay?"

"Tim?"

"Yep."

"Listen, I'm dead tired and befuddled at the moment. Could you come for a visit this weekend? I'll bring you up to date. It would be good to talk to you. I could use a hug."

"I'm your man."

Turning the lights out, she slipped into her pajamas. Watching the street light that shown into her room, she remembered what she had told the men at the bank: a project that will take years to complete. Slow down, girl. It will come in time. With that she drifted off. She dreamt of Tim's coming visit.

CHAPTER 21

Mid-morning, Saturday, Tim pulled up in the driveway. He flipped the car keys in the air then pocketed them. Looking up he saw Sally in the window and gave her a quick wave.

They sat at the kitchen table. Tim listened attentively to the happenings. Then he informed Sally that he couldn't stay. He was to meet his boss in Upper Michigan by supper time.

They had several weeks of work ahead of them, and he wasn't sure when they'd be finished. The lakes up there needed to be tested. There were questions concerning the safety of eating the fish they were pulling from their waterways.

Tim rose from his chair and headed toward the door. Quickly he turned back and took Sally in his arms. They stood there. Momentarily the tenderness passed through their bodies. Kissing her gently on the top of her head, he turned and walked away. "Take care, kid."

The door closed behind him. Sally sank into a chair. There was no energy to rise and see if he turned to wave good-bye. She doubted if he would. She felt like the blood had been drained from her body.

It had been a month since she had seen him. She had marked it up to a busy schedule on both parts.

Were the wonderful feelings from the holidays just a passing emotion? No one had bothered to look for Cinderella to see if the slipper fit.

She didn't know about the rivers and lakes, but her stomach felt like it was full of pollutants.

Tim backed out, then shifted his car into drive. Tracing his earlier route, he ended up at his own apartment in Lansing.

"Sorry, Samuel. I lied to her. What could a fellow like me have to offer a young woman who's inherited a fortune? You asked me to look after Sally, then installed a mountainous money barrier between us."

Tim had been told the story of Samuel and Violet. Now Tim had to deal with the same agony of loss. He refused to shut himself away. Somehow he'd work Sally out of his system. It would be better for both of them. Sure it would.

 CHAPTER 22

It was the last week in February; Sally was still feeling crushed by Tim's departure. She was moving in slow motion. This was getting her nowhere. She must move on. Hurt feelings would have to be dealt with at another time.

Stopping at Webster's office answered some questions. "How did Samuel accumulate that enormous amount of money?"

"You must remember, as a young man he, too, came into a large inheritance. The Witherspoons were well-to-do. Samuel tried to avoid using the money left to him. He basically lived on the money he made from the nursery.

"So in a way you received two suitcases of stacked bills."

"Well, that certainly makes it easier to accept. Really, Webster, whoops, that's supposed to be my secret."

Lloyd laughed out loud. "Now it's our secret. I approve and it makes me feel younger. My wife used to make me laugh with little surprises like that. She's been gone a long time."

He remained quiet for a few minutes then smiled at Sally. "Back to the business at hand. Lake property has steadily increased in value over the years. There were also some wise investments gathering interest.

"I'm sure that Paul has no idea as to the amount of money involved. For some reason, I think he desperately wanted the property. No doubt it would have made him feel like an aristocrat."

Later in the week Sally had Webster legally put a name to the loose ends. Witherspoon, Inc., was established with a P.O. box of its own.

Webster admitted to her that he was retired but too stubborn to give up his office. Besides, he owned the building so didn't have to pay rent. He'd let his secretary go and had cut back on his hours. There were still a few old clients.

A couple of times Sally caught him napping. He'd turn his high-back swivel chair with the back to the door so he could look out the window at the citizens. "Caught me at my favorite pastime, did you?"

"Webster, you're a sweet old thing. I'm glad you waited around for me. You're just the person I need to keep things straight."

"For a compliment like that, I insist on buying you lunch."

They walked to the elevator, and Webster punched a red button. On the fourth floor was a private club Sally was not aware of. She whispered, "I'm not dressed for this."

"Next time I'll let you know in advance. I'm the oldest member. They put up with my idiosyncrasies; plus I'm a big tipper."

As they were being seated, Sally noticed the president of the bank at a nearby table. She smiled sweetly and nodded then turned her attention to Webster.

"I'm sorry, there's no choice. They fix something nice and we enjoy the quiet atmosphere."

Iced tea, a fine chicken salad, delicious dinner rolls, and a scoop of orange sherbet all served elegantly.

"I see no other women. Should I be here?"

"It's a rarity. I noticed the bank president enter the building earlier and heard the elevator. Thought his seeing you here with me would be a lark."

When they returned to Webster's office, Sally kissed him on his forehead. "You're a sweetheart. I'm single, you know, so you'd better beware. Oh no, you're blushing. When are you going to send me a bill?"

"I'm keeping track. Don't you worry." After she left, Webster sat thinking of his Sally. She was nothing like this chipper redhead. But, oh, how he missed her.

Sally went down the list of security system providers in the Yellow Pages. Finally, after phone calls and two personal visits to offices, she settled on the one she was most comfortable with.

What if someone pulled a truck into that out-of-the-way road and emptied the house?

She also called one of the waste companies and ordered two 20-yard roll-off dumpsters, one to be placed next to the house and one between the cottage and the potting shed.

On March 1st Sally was nosing around some out buildings that she and Tim had missed. Pushing open an old garage door, she screamed in delight.

She had no idea the year of the little Ford pickup truck. It was short and compact. The cab was red and the bottom part black. She ran for the house and searched for a desk. There was one in the corner of the living room. There was a file drawer. An insurance folder revealed the fact that the auto was heavily insured. Thank goodness.

Sally called around until she found a reputable person who worked on special antique cars. The owner remembered the truck, having worked on it a few years back.

He was at the gate within the hour. "I want it up to snuff and running. I'd like you to paint, in tiny letters, under the word Ford: Witherspoon,

Inc." The man couldn't help laughing at her because of her excitement.

She ran for the house again. "Hello, Webster. Do you know how to drive a stick shift? Did you know about the little red Ford pickup in a garage out back? When it comes back, I'll come and get you in my car, and you can teach me how to drive it on some back roads.

"When I get good, we'll take it out for a picnic. Whoop! Whoop!"

The elderly man in a dark suit sat in his office with a big grin on his face. "Well, Samuel, she is having fun."

Sally also found some old wooden crates in the garage. She cleaned them up and emptied the papers from the file drawers into them, setting them in the trunk of her car.

This made her realize how careless she had been. There were so many important papers and many valuable items on the property. Anyone could have walked off with things and she would never have known.

The balance of the afternoon was spent rounding up anything she thought should be moved for safekeeping.

The finds today had stirred her blood. It was time to begin. Her brain was whirring.

"Hi."

Sally jumped, then turned around. "Charlotte, you startled me."

"Come for supper."

"Yes, I will. I need to bring you up to date. I'm finished for today. I need to move my car to your driveway. Hop in."

As they ate grilled cheese sandwiches and chili, Sally shared the past week with Charlotte.

"I noticed today there are lots of padlocks on doors, especially on the second floor. Could you clue me in on that?"

"I asked Samuel about that once when I discovered one on a storage closet. He said that, as the years passed, he would go through each room and, if there was nothing in there that he had to deal with, he'd put a lock on the door and forget about the room. Less for him to be concerned about I guess."

"Any keys?"

"I've never seen a set of keys anywhere."

"So each room is a puzzle. I'm beginning to wonder if we'll ever find every piece of this gigantic puzzle. I'm getting anxious to get underway."

On the way home Sally stopped at a hardware store. She told the clerk that she had lost her key to a lock at her house and needed something that would break it open.

CHAPTER 23

Sally had tried to reach Lois all of Monday morning, but her line was busy. Finally about one o'clock she got an answer.

"I've been trying to reach you this morning, Sally."

"The problem was that I was tying up the line calling your number. I know I'm a week early but I'm getting antsy. I was wondering if we could at least set up a date and time for next week."

"How about tonight."

"That's even better."

Arrangements were made for meeting at the big house at six. Lois said that Sally was on the way so she'd pick her up. Charlotte said she'd go over and unlock the back door and put some coffee on.

The kitchen had been modernized several years back, making it a perfect place for the three of them to meet.

Once more Sally tried to convince Charlotte that she should accept pay for her time.

"No, my dear. You two will be doing the real work. I'll be providing forgotten memories and incidentals."

Sally told them what she had looked into so far, and that the business was now called Witherspoon, Inc. She kept the little pickup truck a secret. What fun it would be to spring it on them later.

Lois asked if it would be permissible to set the office up in her house. There was a small room available that was used for storage.

"Set it up to your convenience and get a phone hooked up. Then present me with the bills. Wait. Do you need money in advance? I'm not being very thoughtful, or businesslike."

They were preparing to leave when there were footsteps on a back stairway. Not someone trying to avoid being heard, just slow deliberate steps. A door squeaked, then stillness.

It was then that they realized that each of them had stretched an arm to the center of the table and clasp hands.

"Breathe, girls. I don't believe in ghosts, especially noisy ones. Time to go. We'll drive you home, Charlotte, and go in and make sure there are no intruders. When we leave, lock up tight. Will you be okay?" Charlotte nodded.

After they dropped off Charlotte, Sally and Lois drove to the police station and told the man on duty what had happened.

The officer promised that someone would meet Sally at the property the following morning. They would conduct a thorough search, and he'd have a man swing by during the night.

Sally explained that a security system would be in place before the week was out.

Returning home, Sally called Charlotte for a double check and told her about the stop at the station.

Whoever it was wanted the three of them to be aware of his or her presence. Sally did not sleep well.

The next morning, Officer Harlan appeared. He was young and very thorough. Sally discovered rooms and nooks and crannies that she was not aware of. Eventually, they found where the footsteps probably traveled.

There was a hidden back stairway going up to the attic. At the base was a door heading to the grounds. The opening was behind some shrubs; there were no footprints on the ground. The attic was supporting layers of dust, but the stairway had been swept clean.

"We can dust for prints but I have a feeling that whoever it was knew what he was doing. I'd imagine he used gloves and might have also covered the soles of his shoes.

"I'm not trying to frighten you. Is there anyone who might want to scare you off of the property?"

"I can think of one person, but I can't imagine . . ."

The officer handed Sally a card. "Any more strange goings on, you call me, immediately. My guess is a scare tactic, but why?"

Sally shook her head. Would Paul do such a thing, in hopes of forcing her to abandon the property?

At the next get-together, Sally tried to clear her mind of bad thoughts by telling the girls, jokingly, that she had decided to rent it out at Halloween as a haunted house.

It was an imposing structure and, when evening crept in, it left Sally with eerie feelings. Maybe Edgar Allen Poe resided in one of the padlocked rooms. Maybe there were numerous secret passageways.

There had never been an inkling of this uncomfortable feeling when Samuel was alive. Why now?

Sally thought she could cover her concerns by thinking about Tim. That didn't work. She must avoid thoughts of him. It seemed like such a quick change with no explanation. She must let it go. Fretting about it wouldn't help things, but it still hurt.

Attending church regularly helped. That's when she closed her eyes and forgot the inheritance. On occasions Sally went on one of the singles' excursions. Still the walk home would push the questions to the forefront again.

One morning she received a call from the cemetery office. "I'm sorry, Miss, but artificial flowers are not allowed on the graves."

"I didn't place anything on Samuel's grave."

Sally and Charlotte drove over and met the caretaker. There were three faded cheap plastic flowers stuck haphazardly in the ground.

Sally spoke first. "I know nothing of this."

Then Charlotte. "Nor I."

"You may take it upon yourself to remove any such items." Charlotte nodded in agreement.

Sally commented on the completed marker. Then stated, "I'm not one for visiting cemeteries. I will put something appropriate on the grave on Memorial Day."

"Since I'm close, I'll check now and then, cutting out dead leaves and watching for any other shenanigans. I'm sure that Samuel does not want anyone to spend time here, not even the strange one who visits Poe." This brought forgotten memories to both women.

Sally didn't like the strategies of this lonesome prowler. It was unnerving.

It was time again to refer to the phone book for some help in another department.

Home Inspections

Termites

Demolition Companies

Renovations and Preservation

Building Construction Consultants

Designs and plans.

Sally had cleaned out a lot of the debris in general areas.

On Thursday, March 7th, she met a consultant at the estate. Her immediate concern was the cottage. She had decided to fix it and live there.

Whoever it was that wanted to torment her would find that she was not an easy mark. Whatever the game was, she was determined not to let him win.

The consultant informed her that, left open to the elements for so long, there was no way it could be brought to life. If preserving the idea was important, he would suggest demolishing the structure and starting over. "What did you have in mind?"

"I'd like it to resemble what it must have looked like when it was useful. Openness in the sitting and kitchenette area, a half-bath with shower, and a bedroom big enough for a double bed, a chest of drawers, and a decent closet. Also a tiny screened-in porch with a swing. Plus a storage room that would hold the furnace, water heater, and such."

Writing as fast as Sally talked was difficult. "When would you like this done?"

"Yesterday."

"Excuse me." He stepped away from Sally and was talking into his cell phone. A half an hour passed and Sally was discouraged. He too seemed upset. The last number he dialed was the lucky one. He broke into a big smile. Putting the phone in his pocket, he turned back to Sally.

"How about a move-in date of April 1st?"

"That's an impossible dream."

"One of our local contractors has just let a crew go because building is a bit slow right now. He'd call them back in. What you want is nothing compared to the mansions people want built today. He could have this piece of land cleared tomorrow.

"It's amazing what builders can do now. Very little has to be done from the ground up."

Sally sat down on the grass. "I can't believe this."

The two of them moved on to the big house. "Now this is a different story. This job may take forever. There is a lot of termite damage, water damage, neglect, and old age to deal with. Can we get into these padlocked rooms?"

"We haven't got that far yet. I just wanted you to look at it."

"It can be done. It will take a lot of money, time, and hard work."

With no drum roll, the task of replacing the cottage was begun. Things seemed to be moving along at a surprising pace. On Monday, the 18th, a worker found Sally clearing a room in the big house and asked her to come immediately. In what had been the sitting room of the cottage was a strange sight.

Carefully arranged was a set up for a fire. It wasn't that they had run off before they started it. It was another warning as to how easy it would be.

Sally put a call in to Officer Harlan. He carefully gathered the evidence and put it in the patrol car. "It's someone who knows how to work his way around your security system."

When the crew from the nursery came that afternoon to do some spring cleaning in the yard, Sally pulled one of the older employees aside and made an inquiry. "Is there a security system at the nursery?"

"Sure, Paul knows how to shut it down if he wants to work at night. By the way, he's got himself a lady friend. I've run into them in town several times."

Sally called Officer Harlan and gave him Paul's name and what she knew about him. She didn't want to do it. She did request that the officer be discreet in his inquiries. To accuse the man falsely would be unforgivable.

 CHAPTER 24

The week after the cemetery foolishness, Sally had gotten word to her coworkers from the bank and invited them to a cookout. She did not mention the details of her speedy departure from her job. They thought her new project sounded like more fun.

Lois had contacted some men who were out of work to remove throwaway items from some upstairs rooms. Anything unrepairable ended up in the dumpster. Other pieces of furniture that could be cleaned and fixed were moved to the living room area. The dining area was for stacking any paper items or small furnishings. Passing through the kitchen at the closing of the day, one of the workers mentioned that he had found a dead bat and had deposited him in the trash bin.

This brought Sally to her feet. "Let me find some gloves." She then grabbed the man's hand. "Show me which room you were working in." She was taking the stairs two at a time. He followed behind, wondering, What was the fuss?

Her careful uncovering of the bat and gentle brushing the dust from him produced more confusion.

In turning around, Sally caught a glimpse of the workman's face. Smiling, she winked at him. "Member of the family." The man retreated a couple of steps.

Sally laughed out loud. "If I explained it to you, you would think me daft. So I won't, and you'll still think that. But please come back to work tomorrow. We're not as crazy as we seem."

After he drove away, the lawn crew from the nursery pulled up. The gentleman that Sally had talked to the previous week gave her some additional information.

One of the ladies that he worked with had seen Paul and his lady friend at a local restaurant in November. She had also remarked that the woman was stark looking with little personal appeal.

November, so it wasn't a new friend. She must remember to mention that to Officer Harlan. Maybe that would be a missing piece of the puzzle.

Then he explained that they would come every week to work on the lawns. When Samuel had become ill, he had come up with a figure that he had paid to the nursery for perpetual care.

Sally asked if he knew of Edgar Allan. He assured her that he did. "Well, he was found today, and he too has died. It may sound silly but I salvaged him from a dust bin.

"I'd like him buried on the grounds in an out of the way spot. I have a small box in my apartment. I'll wrap some flannel material around him."

Thoughtfully the man looked around. "How about under the lilac bush?"

"Perfect."

Coming back later that evening, the thoughtful old man and Sally completed their task.

"There, I feel better about that."

The man reached into his work jacket, removed a tiny marker, and stuck it into the ground.

Here lies Edgar Allan,

friend of the family

Sally kissed him on the cheek. "Yes, that will do it. Thank you very much."

"I worked with Samuel for years. I admired him. I think he would be pleased that things were taken care of properly."

Sally was relieved when she got the news that the library was in excellent condition. No physical problems there. It had been built to withstand anything. The family had thought of it as a room full of treasure.

The kitchen was fine, also having been recently refurbished. The first floor had been kept up to date with repairs.

Lois had been born in Greenbriar. Her knowledge was priceless. She was up on who was dependable and honest, and who to steer clear of.

All bathrooms were functional. At this point, they were placed on a later list. They would be updated according to the final decision as to what the house would be used for.

It was time for Sally, Lois, and Charlotte to dig deep in the below-ground area and upper floors. They would do their scavenging during the day when the workers were present.

The last week in March they headed for the basement. There were only a couple of lights, bare bulbs with short pull chains. One, two, three jumps did the trick. They had armed themselves with strong flashlights, which created spooky shadows.

There were some creepy crawly critters. A fruit cellar contained a scattering of Kerr glass canning jars. Whatever was inside was staring back at them, but it was unrecognizable, as was the odor. There were a few jars that had exploded, leaving dried goop on the shelves. A few bugs were embalmed within. It must have been like the old Tarzan movies where the bad guys slowly sunk into quicksand.

The rest of the shelves were collapsing. Spiders had had time to produce magnificent art deco. Sally propped the door open. The balance was open space. It appeared to have an outside entrance.

There was one oversized heavy wooden door. It wasn't locked, but the three of them couldn't budge it. They decided to put it on the waiting list so some strong man could put his muscles behind the shove. Lois wrote down, "Dungeon." Hurriedly, they moved up the stairway. They did find the outside entrance that was to the back of the house. It appeared locked, and they left it that way.

Checking from the outside, they found the typical small basement windows. The one that appeared to be for the room they couldn't gain access to was considerably larger. The windows all were coated with years of grime. Seeing in was impossible; maybe that was a plus.

"Maybe the locked room is storage for wine."

"No, Frankenstein is locked in there."

Sally looked at the two. "You're a lot of help."

As they rounded the corner of the house, they saw Officer Harlan pull into the driveway.

When he reached them he said, "No prints on any of the evidence from the fire set up. Everything could have been purchased at any store. One thing, they carefully removed any stickers showing which store."

Lois left for home to call a bug man to clear out all the vermin, also asking what was the best plan for an old basement with a dirt floor.

Charlotte excused herself and walked toward home.

"Well, so far anyway, he's been meticulous. If he keeps at it, maybe he'll get careless."

The two of them stood, thinking of details that might have been missed.

The officer started shifting his feet. "I was wondering . . . if you'd like to go out for supper tomorrow evening? I'm off duty."

Sally smiled at him. "Now that sounds like a cheerful idea."

"But you can't call me Officer Harlan. My name is Jerry."

Sally smiled again. "I'll work on that. Do you know where I live?"

"Yes, your home address is on the investigative report. Could I pick you up at five? There's a nice place south of here a few miles."

"That will be fine."

With that Jerry turned and walked back to the patrol car.

Sally was delighted. This would give her a day to imagine what he'd look like out of uniform. He couldn't cover up his good looks. Six feet of concern for others, brown hair and eyes, and a sincere smile. His dedication to his job sent out good vibes. He seemed shy, maybe not if you were to know him better. Tomorrow should be a good day.

Sally walked by the cottage on the way to her car. Although it couldn't be ready by the first of April, it was shaping up.

When Sally reached her apartment, she called home and made plans to spend a couple of weeks with her folks. It was time to get away.

After she hung up, the phone rang. It was the man working on the vintage pickup. "She's ready to go, everything is working smoothly." He quoted the figure on the bill.

"I'll put a check in the mail tomorrow. Please hold up on the delivery. I'm going away for a couple of weeks. I'd rather not have it on the property while I'm gone. There have been some strange goings-on out here at the estate."

Sally was told to call when she was back in town. She was wondering if, under the circumstances, she should house it in a safe place and hold off showing it off around the area until the odd happenings came to a halt and the person was caught. Possibly the garage would store it, and she could pay rent. It was a valuable item and a keepsake for sure. One more thing to figure out.

Her date with Jerry was relaxing and fun. Being Tuesday night, business was slow and the atmosphere was subdued, and the background music was turned down to a minimum. The conversation flowed easily.

They held hands while walking back to the car. When they reached Sally's place, he walked her to the door then stood looking at her for a minute. He then said, "I hope we can do this again."

Sally replied, "I had a nice time. Thank you. I'd like that."

Jerry walked down the stairs then turned. "Good night." He closed the outside door behind him.

Sally smiled. It reminded her of the first date in high school: a little awkward, but it left her with bits of memories to ponder.

The following day, the three women started looking into what was behind the padlocked doors. There were several circular staircases. The steps were narrow. People must have been shorter and had smaller feet.

Each of them bumped her head at least once. Squeaky doors, musty smells, and empty spaces: they were disappointed, no surprises. One set of shelves was full of linens yellowed with age.

Thank goodness Samuel had emptied most of the rooms. Some useless items were scattered throughout.

They took time out for lunch. After that they climbed the front stairs. The door at the landing was different from any other. Squirrels and other small animals were carved into the heavy wooden panels. Looking at one another they admitted that this time they felt like they were trespassing.

Sally broke the lock with the bolt cutter she had purchased at the hardware. Slowly, she pushed the door open. They found themselves in a room of long ago. It was Miss Witherspoon's. It had been left untouched, in remembrance.

The large area rugs were of rich golds and browns. The design was indescribable. They questioned crossing the threshold. Carefully, they proceeded. The high canopy bed was of dark wood. The bedcovers and drapes were of heavy pale chamois-colored brocade with intricately embroidered silk leaves. Matching upholstered chairs were arranged in a semicircle around a small table facing the windows. The windows were tall and went to the floor; they opened onto a small balcony.

The view would have been of colorful flower gardens, manicured lawns, and a glimpse of the water. There were rough edges to restore to original beauty. The draperies were tied back to welcome any available light. The ends of the rods were an amber color.

The room was as impressive and classic today as when it was completed originally.

On the other side of the room was a dressing table. The mirror reflected the scarf with painted red roses that was draped across its top. A pearl-handled mirror with matching comb and brush were awaiting the touch of a woman's hand.

Charlotte pulled on the white china handles of the drawer. The three of them gasped and shook their heads. Jewelry.

Because Lila was a woman of height and quality, most of the pieces were of good size. There was a piece of paper tucked in the corner. It was as if she knew whoever found the gems would need help identifying the pieces.

Jade—either of 2 minerals. Jadeite

(most precious) or Naphrite, sometimes

green, used for carving jewelry.

It also means a broken down worthless horse.

That allowed them a pause to laugh and relax.

There was an emerald and a delicate gold locket with a raised rose design. It had a minuscule inscription on the back.

There were two velvet boxes. One contained an exquisite jeweled peacock, the other a violet amethyst that had never been put in a setting.

Sally looked up and found Charlotte rubbing her forehead. "What is it?"

"Now I remember. Samuel said when he was little, there were several peacocks about the place."

"Lois, write that down. What a novel idea. We can look into it, why not?"

Sally left the two to gawk and hurried down to the kitchen, returning with a brown paper bag. "We cannot leave these here." She moved the drawer's contents into the bag and handed it to Lois. "Tomorrow go to the bank and get a good-sized safety deposit box under the company name. I'm sure we'll put it to good use.

"Write a description of what's in here. Make several copies. One for the files in your office and one for each of us. I know nothing of the value, but I do not want any of it lost."

Lois pointed toward the closet door. Hesitating, she finally reached for the decorated knob and pulled the door open. What they saw left them unable to speak. It was full of period dresses. Most were dark colors with a few summer outfits.

Sally found her voice. "You two stay here. I'm off to the hardware. We need a special lock. No one is to know about this room until later.

"I have no idea what to do with it but, for now, nothing is to be disturbed."

When she returned, the girls were excited. "We discovered something else." They pointed to the top of a chest of drawers. "It's an ornate box. We didn't touch it."

Charlotte moved it and lifted the cover. "A music box."

Lois reached behind and wound it. "The Blue Danube" drifted into the room. Sally reached to close the cover. As she did, she noticed the inscription on the inside of the cover.

"To a lovely lady who taught a little black boy how to waltz."

With that she gathered up the box and said, "Follow me."

They climbed to the third floor. Opening double doors, Sally started the music again. It was a ballroom with mirrors on three sides. As the music played, they each imagined a stately woman in a black dress dancing with a small boy. The music stopped and the picture vanished.

Finally Sally was able to speak. "I'm going to keep this at my place for awhile. It seems so sentimental."

She said to Charlotte, "You've kept this room a secret."

"It's no fun without a few surprises."

As they left the house, Sally told Lois and Charlotte she'd be leaving Friday for two weeks with her folks. "Charlotte, you need a break. Keep the men working. Lois, there's plenty of stuff to dispose of inside and out. If you want to give them, and yourself, some time off, do it."

When Sally returned on the twelfth of April, it was late. She unlocked her apartment and found a note and a set of keys on her kitchen table.

You might want to check out your new home. The carpeting you picked out was installed, and the flooring in the bath and kitchen area. We moved the furniture and appliances you had in storage in to make it complete. Probably you'll want to rearrange.

What a swell place.

Sally relocked the apartment and sped to the estate. There was a light on in the cottage. She unlocked the door. A vase of wild flowers sat on the table. What a welcome. It was finished. It was beautiful. It belonged to her. It was her first home.

Sally locked the door, removed her outside clothing, and climbed into bed. It was warm under the blue, yellow, and white quilt that she had purchased in March. She fell to sleep instantly. A contented smile decorated her face.

 CHAPTER 25

Waking early, Sally lay listening to rain washing her windows. It would be easy to slide back into the welcome comfort of her little house. She felt protected.

Slipping into yesterday's clothing, she aimed her car toward her apartment. Unpacking, showering, and donning a clean outfit brought her back to reality. It was good to be back, and she was ready to see if the cleanup work had progressed.

She needed to notify her landlady and pack up her belongings. She could no doubt take care of that tomorrow.

Sally stopped by Lois's office. After hugs and letting Lois know how delighted she was with the cottage, there was a pause that was uncomfortable.

Lois's smile had faded. "One strange thing did occur. I went out the morning after things were put in place. A huge black bow was hanging on the doorknob. It gave me the creeps.

"I called Officer Harlan. He wrote it up. Not a clue. There wasn't a flicker from the alarm, yet it tested out perfect."

Then she started laughing while telling about the night a skunk set off the security system. "Police cars rolled in, lights flashing. Their brights blinded the poor little fella. The officers swore that he grinned at them as he sauntered toward the woods.

"Should you live out there? I'm worried about you."

"I try not to think about it. Whoever it is has done no real damage. I'd be lying if I said it doesn't unnerve me, but more than anything it makes me angry.

"He has easy access, and he's not hiding that fact. I think it's an ego trip, just to see what he can get away with. If he does serious damage . . . well, then." Sally shrugged.

"Don't shrug your shoulders at me. Suppose he sets up something that will include your demise."

Sally raised her hands putting a stop to the discussion.

For once Sally was pleased that she had meager belongings. Sunday she settled in. Details as to what goes where would work themselves out. She'd picked up a pizza on her last trip.

She was lounging in a chair and listening to a new CD she'd picked up while she was at her folks. She got up and turned her player off. There was the noise again, a pitiful cry at her porch door. Turning the outside light on, Sally opened the cottage door. A small kitten was scratching at her porch screen. Not thinking, she bent down to scoop her visitor into her arms.

She watched in horror as a pair of men's shoes rounded the corner of the porch and stood by the kitten.

"I'm lost also. Are you going to invite me in?"

Sally hoped he could not see the panic in her face. Picking the tiny gray baby up in her arms gave Sally a minute to regain her composure. "Of course, Paul, come in."

His crooked smile had her insides churning.

"Have a seat. May I offer you a cup of coffee?"

"No."

There was no attempt at conversation. Paul looked the place over as if he was running a surveillance.

Sally stroked the soft fur to keep her hands from shaking. "Where did you come across the kitten?"

"He was out by the main road. Someone probably dropped him. People can be so cruel. Well, I'll be going now."

"If he is homeless, I can keep him here."

Paul tore the kitten from her hands. "No, you have everything you need. I'll put him back where I found him. He's a little runt. It will do him good to have to have to scrounge for himself."

As he turned to go, Sally noticed a finger of some dark cotton gloves sticking out from one of his back pockets. She was furious. Her anger and courage gave her a strength that was foolish. Her hands clutched into fists.

"Please reset the security system on your way out."

Paul continued to walk away from her. A few more steps and he laughed sadistically.

The gray kitten . . . What would happen to him? Sally shuddered. Sally closed and locked her doors. Her nerves were frayed. She was sure Paul would attempt nothing else this night. In the morning she'd call so the police could add this to the files.

He was getting bold. All she could think about was the kitten. Sally cried herself to sleep.

When she reached Jerry Harlan and explained what happened, he was openly upset with her, as were Lois and Charlotte when they convened. Each of them offered shelter but Sally wouldn't have it.

The scenario had been the same up to this point. Sally feared that the unsettling threats had run their course. Would the danger become real?

Why was Paul open about his involvement? There was no actual proof of any wrongdoing on his part.

Then the odd happenings ceased.

Sally and Lois and a restoration specialist began investigating the extensive work to be done.

The outside stonework was fairly solid. Some patching would be required. The windows with their inside screens and unique hooks were marvelous, but they would have to be scraped and painted each year. The wooden frames were crumbling. It would be impractical to even consider such a plan. Plus it caused an expensive loss of heat in the winter. They must be replaced.

The roof was shingled and covered with moss. It needed to be removed and covered with something more up to date.

The fireplace chimneys were dark. They needed to be checked and cleaned.

The structure needed to be thoroughly checked for termites and the strength of construction.

The inside would come next. Sally felt that painting every room white would be like a cleansing. Then they'd decide where to go from there at a later date. Her preference was to have each room with its own personality. Soft colors would be inviting.

The reconstruction work began in early May. There was constant noise. It would not be a simple task. The thrill made Sally's heart beat faster.

When the house began to show promise there would be the challenge of the outbuildings. Sally had some novel ideas for the potting shed.

Later that month, Sally began riding her bike at the end of each day to change her mindset.

The quiet that existed on weekends was twofold. Sometimes it was a blessing. The flip side was intense silence that cluttered Sally's mind with worrisome thoughts that whirled around in dust swirls.

Coinciding with the plans for the house, Sally decided to go to the public library and search through old newspapers. What was the history of the Witherspoon family and this house? Were they part of the social life of the time?

She had questions about the empty ballroom. One side was windows and three sides mirrors. There was no evidence of chandeliers. Did the room ring with memories and music, or was the atmosphere empty of ghosts? Were there no secrets inside of the walls, no laughter, no sparkling eyes sending messages?

Sally had to know.

It was the last Saturday in May before she found time to stand before the information desk and inquire about back papers.

Her eyes were tired. As far as she could tell, this was not a family for socializing. There was no mention of the ballroom. Sally sat in front of the computer with her eyes closed. When she was finished, there would be lively activities at the estate.

The ballroom would be fabulous and periodically used for memorable evenings of dance. Such a place would come alive, she'd see to it.

"Are you asleep or dreaming?" She was afraid to look up.

"Tim?" She did not know what to say. It had been a very long time.

"Charlotte told me where to find you. It looks like things are coming along out at the estate."

"There's lots to do. It will be a long time yet." She wished he would move closer. Her heart strings were taut. Trying to forget Tim had been impossible. Her smile was weak and troubled. Why was he here?

Over his shoulder another face appeared.

"Hi. Charlotte told me you were here and maybe you'd like a lift home."

"Tim Crawford, Jerry Harlan."

They nodded at each other.

"I've got to be going. I was passing this way and thought I'd see how things were going for you." Tim gave a casual wave, and he turned and walked down the stairs.

Sally took a deep breath.

"Would you like a lift?"

"That would be kind of you."

Sally slipped her jacket on and gathered her things.

No words were exchanged. Jerry held the car door for her, knowing that her thoughts were elsewhere.

Jerry pulled up by the cottage leaving the motor running. Sally got out. Leaning down she simply said, "Thank you."

"No goodnight kiss?"

"Not tonight, okay?" Sally walked slowly to her door, used her key, and entered. She didn't turn any lights on, but sat down in a chair, feeling like an empty shell.

Jerry headed back to town. The evening had uncovered a fact that he was not aware of.

Tim's drive to Lansing turned out to be a long lonely ride. Why had he stopped, what had he wanted?

Charlotte knocked on the door of the big house Sunday morning. There was no answer, but Sally was sitting at the table. Charlotte reached in her pocket for her emergency key. Walking past Sally she fixed coffee, poured a glass of orange juice, and put bread in the toaster.

"Good morning."

Sally looked up. "Sorry."

"Did I do wrong?"

"No. I'm confused. I don't know what's the matter with me. Thanks for breakfast. Join me?"

"I've eaten, thanks. Cry if you like."

That forced a smile from Sally. "Would that solve the problem?"

"Not really. Love problems are not easily solved. Eventually it will work itself out."

"Promises. Promises."

 CHAPTER 26

June first, Jerry called Sally, finally getting around to the question he wanted answered. "I wondered if you'd like to take in a movie?"

"Sounds good."

Sighing with relief he continued, "There's a new ice cream place in town. You been there yet?"

"Nope, but that sounds doubly good."

The movie was senseless. When they entered the ice cream parlor, there were whispers behind the counter. One of the young ladies spoke up. "Hi Jer, your usual?"

While keeping a straight face, Sally could see that this was going to be more entertaining than the flick. She mouthed, Jer, your usual.

Jerry's face turned a bright red.

Since she was a first-time customer, they explained the routine. What fun. While fixing their order, the girls broke into a cute little ditty.

It brought smiles to the customers' faces. Someone whispered, "I thought they didn't do that unless you put a tip in the jar on the counter." Sally smiled again and nudged Jerry. As the door continued to open, Jerry and Sally slipped out.

Laughter had control of Sally, and she could hardly eat her chocolate ice cream with a peanut butter cup mixed in. She loved waffle cones.

Jerry pleaded, "Will you stop that?"

Which only made things worse. She linked arms with him when they were finished.

"They are too young for me."

"Are you sure? The one in charge was openly studying you. I don't think they were happy that you brought a friend."

Jerry stopped short. "Is that all we are, friends?"

The fun atmosphere had evaporated.

"I wish I knew the answer to your question."

They walked the rest of the block in a stiff silence.

"I'm sorry. The library . . . What about him?"

"I don't know about that either."

They had cut through the little park by the bank. Jerry stopped and took Sally in his arms. Sally leaned her head against his chest.

"I wish I knew where I fit into your life. I'm not saying I want to get serious, but I feel special when I'm with you." Laughing softly he said, "I don't want to die of a broken heart."

"I don't either. Can we leave it at that for now?"

She pushed away from him. He drew her back and kissed her lightly.

When Sally arrived home she wrote a letter to her folks. She passed on information about Charlotte and her friend, telling that a lot of their time was spent on bike trails, and how he could be seen repairing old steps or digging out dead bushes.

Also she mentioned Lloyd Webster. How he had called to see if she still lived in town. She had to explain why she had not gotten back to him about driving with a stick shift. Her dad would love the little pickup.

He knew of it but she'd saved the details. Sally could hardly wait until it would be safe to have it delivered.

Then she talked of Lois, her husband and daughter, and how they were off to horse shows. Still she was keeping all paperwork up to date and bills paid, and Sally could reach her by company cell phone if questions came up.

Her last paragraph was the one she was most proud of. Sally invited them to come for a visit. She was anxious to have them check out the progress. They knew there was no extra room in the cottage and that the big house was not livable yet. She spoke of a bed and breakfast close by that had recently opened. Her favorite part was that she'd make reservations, and it was on her. That would be a first.

She got up from the chair and bounced around the room making up silly cheers. It felt good to be independent. She so often thought of Samuel and the gift he had given her. At times it was still hard to comprehend something as vast as this. She hoped she was living up to his expectations. Sally often felt like she should take him on a tour: This way Samuel, see what I've done here. Then she'd smile, because she often felt his presence. It was comforting knowing he was about. She hoped he was elsewhere when the visitor played his tricks.

Next time the group came from the nursery, Sally cornered them. She was excited about what might be done to prepare the cottage for the yard she had in mind. Paul was to be bypassed. Could they do it without his supervision? She'd pay full price for the job. Avoiding him was important to her. Showing them a picture from a magazine got them interested for sure. They'd report back the following week.

The cottage was settled. The month of June was slipping by fast.

Jerry and Sally had driven to Pentwater on Sunday, the 16th, and spent the day. When they returned he made sure she was locked in the cottage with the lights on. Working the early shift the following day pushed him to head home earlier than he liked.

CHAPTER 27

Sally sat down to go through yesterday's mail. Within minutes the cottage lights went out. In the distance she caught a glimpse of Charlotte's lights. The two were on the same line so it was not a power outage.

She lifted the phone; dead.

Sally felt like she was in a cave, deep and dark. The stillness overpowered her.

Remembering that her cell phone was in her purse she felt her way to the table. Dialing 911, she reached the station. She stated her name and whereabouts. Talking to someone made her feel somewhat better.

The emergency person informed her that there were two officers cruising in the vicinity.

Sally said, "There is a flashlight darting around in the woods."

One of the officers was on the line. "Lock up and sit tight. We are leaving the car and heading your way."

"Wait!"

"What is it?"

"There are more than one. There are two lights. They are moving about blinking the lights off and on like fireflies.

"They want to make sure I see them. They are shining the lights toward each other. They are letting me see their silhouettes. From the distance I'd guess they are wearing dark clothing.

"They must know you are close because they've doused their lights."

The cottage lights came on, blinding Sally, and she fell to the floor.

One of the men searched the grounds. The other officer was calmly asking Sally to unlock her door.

In the meantime, Jerry had been reached and was picking up the conversations. Making a U-turn, he was driving back toward the lake. He had just let her off. This couldn't go on. Whoever it was had gone too far.

Sally was trembling. The one officer stepped through the doorway and right behind him was Jerry. The third man came in, reporting that the phone wires were cut.

All three echoed, "You are not staying out here alone." One said, "If we have to we'll take you into police custody."

Sally shook her head and pronounced an emphatic no. "They won't come back tonight. The pranks had stopped so I had false hope that the game was over. Tomorrow one of you can go to Mr. Webster's office with me. He is my lawyer. He and I can give you more information. I didn't want to falsely accuse anyone. There are some additional things you should know."

Jerry suggested she stay with Charlotte for the night. Again a stubborn no.

"Officers, you were the first on the scene. Arrest this woman and take her to the station for her protection."

They each took an arm easing Sally toward the door. The look she gave Jerry was lethal.

"You can't do this."

"If you have to, cuff her, gentlemen."

Sally stormed out of the cottage with a cloud of steam above her head.

"Put her in a cell for safekeeping. Better give her two blankets. We need her to be as comfortable as possible. I hear she likes cinnamon toast for breakfast. I'll call a couple of people who need to know her whereabouts."

Sally wouldn't look at him.

"You will be safe locked up. We can keep an eye on you tonight. Tomorrow some other arrangements will be made. These pranks, as you call them, have no humor."

The officers escorted her to the cruiser. In the night they heard her crying. Was it from embarrassment or fear?

Jerry lay in his own bed wondering if he had ended a friendship of someone he cared about a great deal. He hoped not. It wouldn't be an easy situation to mend, that's for sure. Most important, he did not want anything to happen to her. What he had done was drastic, but Sally had to understand that any of these incidents could become out of control, deadly.

 CHAPTER 28

The following morning, Sally was driven home so she could shower and change. After that the officer drove her to Lloyd Webster's office. On the way in, he explained that Officer Harlan would be waiting inside for her.

She was hoping to avoid him, but he was seated across from Webster. She greeted the lawyer kindly enough, only giving Jerry a disgusted look.

Webster motioned for her to take a seat. Then he did something that startled her. "Young lady, Officer Harlan has explained your housing situation last evening. You should be grateful. I suggest you thank him . . . with a smile on your face."

He had no smile on his face as he addressed her. "Do it!"

Sally blinked. She was taken aback. Webster leaned forward. "Follow my instructions."

Sally scowled and squeaked out a meek thanks without looking in Jerry's direction.

The lawyer placed his arms on his desk. "Listen closely. It's time you grew up. You think no one is going to hurt you. Welcome to the real world. Someone is trying to destroy you, mentally.

"I should take you to the woodshed and shake the puddin' out of you. Do you understand what I'm saying?"

Sally slid further back in the chair. "Yes, Sir."

"I thought highly of you. At the moment you remind me of a spoiled little girl."

Sally wanted to cry. Both of these men were special friends. She lowered her head in shame. "I'm sorry."

"You should be. Lecture is over. I suppose you came here so we could tell this fine officer what happened the day of the reading of the will."

"Yes. I thought he needed to hear it from two viewpoints."

Sally and Webster left out nothing. Jerry shook his head. "Why didn't you come forward with this information before?"

Sally spoke up. "It was my fault. Sometimes the obvious person is not the guilty party."

"You should have let us worry about that angle. I'll include it in my report. Now we need to figure out what to do with you."

Webster raised his index finger. "I have a possible solution. My wife passed away years ago. I live alone at the end of this block. Cars go by at all hours so I am protected from any vandalism. There is a guest room with private bath. I would be honored if this young woman would brighten my doorway." Eyes and smile were sending wicked signals. Then he laughed. "I'm a bit past my prime so she'd be safe. You could go about your business during the day and, say, maybe I could talk you into fixing a few home-cooked meals."

Sally was mulling this over. She looked at Officer Harlan and nodded.

The officer looked at the lawyer. "It's a done deal. You are also right around the corner from the station in case I have to keep an eye on you, Sir. One question, can she have callers?"

Webster squinted his eyes. "As acting uncle, I would have to scrutinize her visitors, of course."

Officer Harlan and Sally walked down to the police van, and he drove her home to get her car. Jerry said, "Can you ever forgive me?"

"Sounds like if I don't I'm going to have to pay a fine."

She rounded up some belongings and moved them to Webster's. He had given her a key to a side door. It was a nice old house set up for the lawyer's everyday comfort. Sally stepped out the back door and picked a bouquet from among the weeds by the side of the house, then put it in a glass.

As she filled it with water, she noticed that it had a picture of Mickey Mouse on the front. When she left to go to Lois's office, she saw how dry Webster's grass was. Yes, there were some ways she could repay him for his kindness.

On Wednesday, Sally picked up some hanging baskets and perennials at the farmer's market. She couldn't seem to get enough bright colors around her. She'd save one of the baskets for Webster.

She'd saved a few to plant at the far end of the potting shed. If, in the long run, she'd change its structure, she'd transplant them.

She had gathered her tools and a few flats and began loosening the ground in the area. She didn't want to leave all the beautification for the nursery staff.

It was a perfect day for working outside. Turning the earth had Sally smiling. She began to sing.

One of the workers at the house tilted his head, then motioned for his coworkers to stop and listen.

"Oh, what a beautiful morning. Oh, what a beautiful day! I've got a wonderful feeling everything's going okay."

She lifted and turned over another shovelful of dirt. She stepped back.

Hesitantly, she reached down with her garden glove and carefully moved some dirt around. She stood up, studied the ground, and bent again.

Working with her hands, she followed the outline, gently sorting through more dirt.

Straightening up, she took a deep breath. Then she ran toward the house. When she entered the kitchen, she slammed the door and locked it, as if it would be a barrier for the monsters. Were they ever going to leave her alone?

She had stopped her singing abruptly. The men then saw her scrambling for the house and heard the slam of the door.

Puzzled, they returned to work until the police cars started rolling in.

 CHAPTER 29

Reaching for the phone, Sally dialed 911. When the call was answered, she was embarrassed to speak her name. The folder pertaining to her and this property must be bulging. Slouching in a kitchen chair, she told of finding a skeleton buried in a shallow grave by her potting shed.

The voice assured her there would be an officer there promptly.

Sally heard the police car pull up by the back door. She went out to meet the young officer, and they walked toward the potting shed.

One quick look and he was on his phone. "We'll need a medical examiner, a detective, and an evidence technician out here. I'm putting yellow tape up enclosing the immediate area and more farther out.

"I think you should locate Officer Harlan. He's the one who has been in charge of the case out here. This may be a separate thing from what he's working on, but he should be notified."

Turning toward Sally, the officer reached out to steady her. "Let's find a place for you to sit." The closest thing was a stump. He'd read Harlan's reports about this case. No wonder this young woman was shaky.

When Jerry arrived, he hurried to Sally. "You okay?"

She gave a half smile. "From one to ten?" Exhaustion was encompassing her body.

He wished he could take her in his arms, but he touched her on the shoulder, then turned to talk to the other officers.

Sally called home to warn her folks about possible news coverage of the latest problem. Her sister answered and started talking before Sally could get a word in.

"I was just going to call you, Sally." Shirley, Sally's ten-year-old niece, had been wanting to come for a visit. They were thinking of dropping her off on the 20th and picking her up on Saturday the 22nd. Shirley's dad was going through the area on business, and her mom was planning to accompany him.

Finally, Sally relayed her message. The timing was grossly wrong. "Maybe it will be good for me to have something else to think about. We can call it her mystery weekend. She'll learn a lot in three days."

Yellow tape had been placed across the entry road. Sally informed the officer in charge of the expected arrival of her sister and family the following day.

Although the police had tried to keep things under wraps, the information had leaked out. The night of the 19th, the county mounted police had been called in to make sure no curiosity seekers entered the property by way of the water or the woods and disturbed anything.

A policeman was stationed at the entry road to keep the public and news media off the property and away from Sally. Now and then a new TV station would be added to the crowd. They'd call out, "What was her reaction when she first saw the skeleton?" The same foolish question. The officer would shake his head.

When Shirley arrived near noon, Sally's sister was shocked. "Wow, Sis, this is big-time stuff." Even at that, a quick wave and they were gone.

Sally looked at Shirley. "Does anything deter your mother from her own plans?" Shirley laughed and hugged her aunt.

"It's been on TV ever since it happened, but you know Mom. If it's not happening to her . . ."

Before dark, the preliminary testing was done and the remains were removed from the estate.

Shortly after, Sally and Shirley, huddled on the floor of the back seat of one of the cruisers, made it safely to Webster's.

Webster drove the girls to an old country store about ten miles away for ice cream. On the way Sally was explaining to Shirley about the mounted police being involved.

Webster asked Shirley, "Are you having fun so far?" The three of them laughed, but it wasn't happy laughter.

On the 21st, the nursery crew arrived to work on plantings surrounding the cottage. Shirley came into the kitchen of the big house, which was the center of things. Some man named Paul had asked if she'd like to go to the zoo in Grand Rapids this afternoon. She told him he'd have to check with her aunt. "I used that excuse to get away from him. He was twitchy."

"Twitchy?"

"You know." She demonstrated with some odd little moves. It wasn't funny but Sally laughed.

Sally instructed Shirley to stay in the house. She'd take care of it.

"I guess that's a no, huh? There's so much happening here I'd rather stay where the action is." Shirley's visit was proving good medicine.

Sally took a shortcut to the cottage. Paul was not director-in-chief, but he was checking things out.

"Good morning, Paul. My niece is tied up with activities the short time she's here."

"It was just a thought. Are you satisfied with this crew? I want to make sure our customers are happy."

"They are more than satisfactory." Sally turned and abruptly walked away. Paul made some remark about the Wednesday news but Sally didn't acknowledge it.

Sally slammed the kitchen door. "You're right, Shirl, twitchy."

When Shirley's folks picked her up it was dusk. They had a quick tour of the estate, all the time telling of their good time. "All we heard on the car radio was about the spooky stuff going on here."

"If you have any questions, Shirley will be glad to fill you in on details."

As they started to drive away Sally called, "Love you, Shirl girl," and blew her a kiss. "Write to me."

Now there were other disasters on the news.

Sally arrived at Webster's. He had waited to fix her hot tea. She slept until noon on Sunday. Wonderful smells were filling the house. Sally slipped into her robe and headed for the kitchen.

Webster had on an apron and he was making gravy. Sally walked up behind him and touched his arm. "Webster, you are a very kind person."

No one had said words like that to him in a long time. It was a moment to savor.

CHAPTER 30

That old house didn't have an automatic dishwasher, which gave Sally and Webster an opportunity long gone out of style.

Two people, time to talk, time to listen. Functioning as a team was a healthy maneuver that brought strength to a friendship.

Afterward, Sally curled up on the sofa, and Webster was rocking in his favorite chair.

"I know you're tired, Sally, but I wonder if you could give me a sketch of this latest complication. I may have to be your legal consultant on this one."

"I was preparing to plant some perennials by the potting shed. Someone had planted a body in the same spot. It was a shallow grave. It sounds simple enough, but it plays tricks with your mind."

She paused, attempting to keep the facts in order.

"The people at 911 are beginning to recognize my voice." Sally shook her head.

"In minutes a policeman was there. I was surprised to learn that a medical examiner has to come before anyone else can proceed, even when it's a skeleton. His job is to make sure they are human bones and issue a death warrant.

"Detectives were pulling in like it was a car rally, followed by the mobile vehicle with the evidence technicians and their equipment. They work closely with the anthropology department at Michigan State."

Sally began to shake her head as if trying to erase a bad dream.

"Eventually, they figured that it was a dump sight; that it happened elsewhere. Soil samples were gathered. Did you know that maggots don't waste a day to begin their work?"

Sally shuddered. She could remember the summer she spent on the farm. She'd helped her granddad dip his sheeps' hooves in a solution to rid them of maggots. She shuddered again.

It brought to mind that she had read that during the Civil War, doctors placed maggots in badly infected legs to clean out the infection.

Sally fell to the floor and lay flat out. Webster rushed to her side. She shook her head no. "I feel so sick. Just let me be." Closing her eyes, she took a deep breath. The room was circling around her.

The doorbell rang. Webster hurried to answer it in hopes that it was someone who could assist him. Grabbing Jerry Harlan's sleeve, Webster yanked him into the room.

Jerry rushed toward Sally and got down on his knees beside her.

Webster explained, "The skeleton and how quickly a body starts decomposing; the maggot business."

Jerry sat back on his heels. "Things are catching up with her, and she's had enough.

"Sally, go put on some loose-fitting clothes. You and I are taking a ride in the country. It's a fine night. You need some fresh air. We'll ride with the windows open and let your hair blow. We won't talk."

Sally pulled herself up to a sitting position and reached for Jerry's hand. The tears flowed. Gradually, the well ran dry. She rose and headed to her room.

"She was giving me the lowdown on this last mess." Webster told Jerry where she had left off. Jerry filled him in on a few more details.

"They use sift boxes going thoroughly through the soil layer by layer. It's important that they keep the skeleton intact as it is found. Their guess is that it may be a teenager.

"Two weeks, two months, the bones can be bare. It depends on the soil and the weather. It's possible this one has been there a while."

As soon as Sally appeared, Jerry took her hand, and they headed for the car. They had barely left the street lights behind when she had relaxed and was sleeping soundly, as he had thought. Slowing his speed, he smiled. This would be good for her.

The following day there was a knock on the kitchen door of the big house. Sally was at the table organizing paperwork to take over to Lois's. T.T. ambled through the door and sat down across from her.

"I'd like a few minutes of your time, Sally."

"Not even one minute until you tell me what your initials stand for."

"Tobias Tyler. Toby Tyler, you know the little kid who ran away with the circus."

"Truth?"

"Afraid so. Hardly a good handle for a grown man."

Sally put the pile she had been working on in a brown envelope.

"I wanted to speak to you about the dead body."

Sally bristled. "That's a police matter. It doesn't concern me. They are handling it. They suspect it happened a while back."

"I am a retired police officer, and I have a hunch about a possible identification."

"Oh, I didn't know that. Why don't you talk to the men at the station?"

T.T. sighed. "The force don't like it when an old grudge like me thinks he can solve a current case. I'd like to run my idea past you to see what you think."

He had been a detective when a drunk driver had hit his police car and mangled his leg. When he had recuperated, he was in the same department but assigned to a desk.

He claimed that a few years back, a father came in wanting help finding his daughter who was fifteen. Later that day, his wife had got a ride in from the fields. She was spittin' mad. She'd yelled at everyone in the station. She wanted them to know that the girl was young but had the body of a woman. Words flew around the room, loose morals, a foul mouth, lazy. Good riddance. It was an itinerant family with several youngsters. They were ready to move on. One less mouth to feed would be good. The mother was sure the girl had run off with some man.

The information had been filed.

"I have a feeling that these may be the bones of that girl. If it is her, I'd like her to know that someone cared."

Sally remained quiet for a long time.

"Why come to me?"

"I have a hunch that I know who did it. It's a long shot, but my gut says, don't walk away from this. Somewhere hidden in the files, or in my memory, is information that others will miss."

"Are you willing to clue me in on who you think the guilty party is?"

T.T. squirmed. They were staring at each other. Then he blurted out, "Paul Kline."

Sally sat chewing at the end of a pencil. "Why?"

"I stopped by the nursery a couple of days later to order some black dirt delivered. Paul knew who I was. The missing girl didn't make the paper but the gossip floated through the town.

"The man was a truck load of nerves. He almost fell twice, tripping on bags of mulch. Before we had completed our business, he had called over another salesperson and stumbled toward the restroom."

"That's not much to go on. Maybe he was ill. You were no doubt trained to see things that I don't but . . ."

"I'll need to know about forensic findings. It's logical that you would inquire, and they would keep you up to date on things."

"You and I may end up in jail, T.T., with this underhanded stuff."

"I sound crazy suggesting this, I know. I want someone to know what I'm attempting to do in case something goes wrong. Trust me."

"T.T., you're scaring me. This sounds like a cheap novel."

He'd gone.

Sally was frightened by his visit. She knew little about Charlotte's friend. This was beginning to feel like a train that was trying to run on a disengaged track.

When Sally stopped at Lois's office, she plopped herself in the easy chair. "One quick question: Do you think we are all going insane?"

"You've been working too hard. I think it's tea time. Come on in the TV room. Hubby collects old Charlie Chan movies and converts them to run on our DVD."

"No! I'm not staying. I'm heading for a long bike ride. Thanks anyway."

On her way back home she came upon the young man in his wheelchair whom she'd seen before. "Hey, how've you been doing?"

"Things are looking up. I've been hired as a private investigator."

"Can't talk anymore." Sally mumbled. "I've got to get home."

The whole world is going mad. Sally peddled fast to see if she could escape.

CHAPTER 31

The clock radio woke Sally at seven with the announcer reminding her that it was July first. It was drizzling rain so she decided to loll about, knowing that the weather wouldn't deter Webster from his lengthy early morning walk.

Wishing that yesterday had been written in chalk would allow her to erase the board and also to erase it from her mind.

Propping her pillows up behind her back, Sally decided to see if running happenings through her thinking process would put things into perspective.

Paul, when she and Samuel had visited the nursery she would have guessed Paul to be in his late forties, early fifties. Later she knew him to be in his early forties.

He reminded her of Basil Rathbone from those old movies of the '30s and '40s that she had watched on TV. He was not bad looking, but his pallor was so white, it appeared that he had been made up with flour. He had the mustache, prominent nose, dark eyes, and early graying sideburns. He appeared troubled and gave the impression of not feeling well; stomach problems from poor eating habits and lack of food. An undercurrent existed that made Sally feel uncomfortable. Could he have committed a crime in years past? Was T.T.'s involvement good or bad?

This brought her to the point where she needed to be. Worrying about the police and its case was a waste. It was not her problem.

Her job was to fulfill Samuel's dream of turning a rundown piece of property and crumbling buildings into something usable and radiating with beauty.

Hopping out of bed, she hurried into the shower. She was dressed and had homemade pancakes ready to serve up when Web walked through the back door.

"Do I see a smile on that pretty face?"

"Time to move on, Webster."

"Since you cooked, I'll do the dishes."

"Good deal. I'm off then."

As Webster picked up the dishes, his mind could not sway from thoughts of his Miss Gordon. He adored her vibrant personality. He doubted that she was aware of her genuine appeal. Ah, to be young again.

The man who courted and won her had better be worthy. He was too old to slay a dragon, but he would guard her with his life.

Any day now she would move back to her little house. His home would return to its echoes of the past. He was not anxious for her departure.

The ringing of the phone startled him. Shuffling across the room, he picked up the receiver.

"Webster, old buddy, come out to the big house. There is someone here that's going to put some zip in your life. Half an hour, get a move on."

He stared at the phone. Picking up his pace, within minutes, he was driving toward the lake. Once again Sally had stirred his imagination.

When he arrived, Sally came out to meet him. "When I got here, this snazzy red convertible was in the drive. I tracked down its owner. She was buzzing through the house with a yellow pad. Ideas were being listed and drawings filled any empty spaces.

"She's a friend of my mother, an interior decorator. She's nice and her ideas are super. My problem is I need to get to work, and I don't have time to take her to lunch."

Sally looked at Web hopefully. "I thought maybe you could take her to your club. Maybe out to supper this evening also."

Web scowled. This kind of tactic was not like Sally.

At that moment, a woman stepped out the back door. Her smile was mesmerizing. She wore a pale summer pantsuit that highlighted her figure and good looks. She moved toward him like a model. She wore no jewelry and fashionable but comfortable-looking shoes.

Webster stood taller and straightened his tie.

"Celia Clark, Lloyd Webster. You can call him by his last name, Webster, or Web. Please don't call him Lloyd."

Sally doubted that either of them heard what she said.

Webster offered Celia his arm and started toward the passenger side of his car. "I'd like to give you a tour of our little town." He turned back. "After work you go home and get dressed, and we'll all go to dinner to some place special."

Before they went to lunch, Web stopped at his office. "Enjoy the view of downtown through my picture window. It's important that I make a couple of calls." He quietly closed the door to his inner office.

When he returned Celia was sitting in his chair holding her legs out straight and twirling around. When she faced him, she turned pink. Her laughter sounded like delicate wind chimes.

It was just short of six when the three of them arrived for dinner and were shown to their table overlooking the lake. "Table for six as you ordered, Mr. Webster." Sally glanced at Webster. Coming in right behind them were Charlotte and T.T.

"Your escort is going to be a few minutes late, Sally."

As they were drinking coffee, Sally caught a reflection in the window glass that shocked her. Slowly she turned and stared. She had expected Jerry.

"How . . . ?"

"There are ways. Maybe you should greet him."

Sally stood slowly. Her linen napkin slid to the floor. Gliding across the room was done in slow motion. She reached toward him with both hands. He enclosed her hands in his. "It's been a while, Tim."

"It has. Is this okay?"

"Yes, of course."

Their orders were taken, and Sally still didn't know how to react.

Tim reached for her hand under the table as if to reassure her. He knew her well.

Tim left first because of his drive home. After Sally was dropped off by Web, she lay awake until he returned from seeing Celia to her motel. The digital numbers on the clock showed that it was after twelve. It had been an enjoyable evening with friends. Was it any more than that? What did she want it to be?

When asked about her plans for the fourth, Sally promptly answered, none. She would rest, sleep, take a lazy day. Her energy level was below zero.

On the 5th, Jerry stopped by with some news. At the scene they had found a red leather strap shoe underneath where the right leg was twisted beneath the body. There were some rivets that could be from jeans. Also a broken necklace.

"You look beat, Jerry."

"Yesterday was long. The 4th is a party day. Drunk drivers. Bad accidents. I'm off at three. Hope to catch up on some rest.

 CHAPTER 32

T.T. had seen the police car drive past Charlotte's as he mowed her lawn. Even the riding mower bothered his leg. When finished, he painfully worked his way to the big house and Sally. His knock on the screen door was weak.

Sally was not surprised to see him. She poured iced tea for each of them. "I'm sure Charlotte is not going to like you less if you don't do her yard work."

"I want her to think I'm still alive and kicking."

Sally smiled. "How's the special-designed bike working?"

That perked T.T. up a bit. "By gosh, I'm impressed. Plus Charlotte insisted that I go to rehab regularly. I was lax about it after the accident, which makes it doubly hard now." Hanging his head but grinning, he said, "There are reasons to feel good now."

Sally passed on the information Jerry had delivered. "Don't tell me what you are going to do with what I've told you. I don't know if that makes me less guilty, but . . . One question, the young man with the wheelchair."

T.T. stopped her there. "I've used him before. He's sharp but looks harmless. He goes everywhere in town. It embarrasses me to complain about my leg. He lives in the same neighborhood as Paul." Taking a long drink of his tea he continued. "He goes by Paul's house often, only now he notices things that he ignored before." He did not tell Sally what he and the young fellow had uncovered.

A pair of binoculars had proven to be worth the price. After dark a person in black pants and hooded sweatshirt could move in the shadows of a tree-lined street without being spotted.

At the back of Paul's rental house property was a garage. It was windowless with rotting paintless wood, leaning to the left. A hard blow would take it down.

Maybe that was why Paul would check it every night at nine. He'd remove a key from his pocket, open the padlocked side door and look inside.

One evening Paul arrived home late. He parked his '93 Jeep Grand Cherokee Laredo next to the side door of the house.

The wheelchair was tucked behind some shrubbery, allowing the young man to see things from a different angle. As Paul unlocked the door to the garage, a gust of wind whipped it from his hand. While he struggled with it, a pair of binoculars, with the help of a streetlight, caught a glimpse of a car inside. A smile creased the face half-hidden by a black hood.

T.T. had called in some favors at the station and had received a copy of the original short file on the missing girl.

One item had him encouraged: the reported necklace. He remembered her father's solemn face. He had given his daughter a heart-shaped necklace on her last birthday, and she had never taken it off. He thought maybe that could be one way they could identify her.

The sadness was the family did move on. The girl might have known where they were heading and rejoined them later. There was nothing final in the write-up and no way to trace them. The report had been filed in '95.

By the following Monday, T.T. was rattled. He'd heard that the investigation was not going well. The chief always greeted him kindly, but that day he could feel his frustration.

When T.T. shared some of his information with him, he was disgruntled.

"You're retired, remember?"

"This case means something to me for a variety of reasons. I want to help. If I am right, it will close the book on this one."

Before the chief sat a man with years of experience. Paper-wise he was retired, but his mind was still churning out facts and wise advice. According to forensics and anthropology, the fifteen-year-old girl had been buried seven years before. The chief didn't want an unsolved crime in the files.

"Tell me everything you've got." So the two of them forgot the rules and discussed the case.

"I'll obtain a search warrant for the property where Paul lives. We'll stop by the nursery just to talk to him. See how he reacts when we serve the warrant."

The next morning, ten minutes after the nursery opened for business, a police car rolled into the parking lot. The chief and the old cop with the limp walked toward the office. Paul looked up and they were standing in his office doorway.

The phone in his hand fell to the desk. The look on his face was one of despair. Regaining his composure instantly was not soon enough. It had registered clearly in the minds of the two men. The chief stepped forward and laid the warrant on Paul's desk. Casually, he said, "Would it be okay if we asked you a few questions?"

Paul opened the envelope and read the typed page. "What's the meaning of this?"

"We're working on an old case and thought maybe you could help us out."

Paul looked at his watch. "I'm sorry but I have a delivery to make. Possibly another time." He ushered them out.

They were climbing back in the cruiser when they saw Paul in the driver's seat of the Nature's Nursery van racing out the rear driveway.

Taking off after him, they called into service a backup team to go to Paul's house.

Seeing a police car in his driveway didn't stop him. Frantically, he drove across the lawn toward the garage. Jumping out, his car rolled into the back fence.

Paul stood in front of the side door to the garage. Surrounding him were men of the law. They waited and watched.

"Gentlemen, my personal prison for seven years."

Then Paul man crumbled and fell in a heap in front of them.

The chief called 911. Paul was taken to the hospital under police guard. An arrest warrant would be issued. Everyone moved around in silence. Even though Paul was a suspect, watching a man completely fall apart was disturbing. No one handled it well.

The car was removed to the police garage. After much searching, they discovered a dark strand of hair caught in some tangled electrical wiring and a spot of blood under some dirty rags. Near the spare tire there was a thin piece of leather strap with the golden hook still clasp together.

That Friday, Paul was moved to the jail. They left him alone over the weekend to see what would happen.

Monday, Sally, Webster, and T.T. were seated in an adjoining room. They could observe through the special glass and could hear the proceedings.

This was not the broken man they had picked up. Paul was back to his usual nasty self.

"Now, we have some questions that need answers."

"What are you accusing me of? What right have you to hold me?"

"We are detaining you as a suspect in a death that took place seven years ago."

"I didn't murder her."

The room went silent. The interrogator waited. He did not raise his eyes from the paper on the table. It was as if no one was breathing.

Paul yelled, "Stop it! I hate your tricks. You think you're so clever."

Watching Paul's facial changes was frightening.

"You should have seen her. Everyone had gone home. She was waiting by my car. I'd noticed her several times. She'd bummed a ride in with some of the other workers when they had been sent in to pick up supplies. She'd watch me.

"Low slung skin-tight jeans, no bra under her skimpy top. Lots of soft skin open for the touching. Sexy red strap spike heels. She was giving me a come-on smile."

He put his fingers to his hairline and began to massage his forehead.

"I was thirty-seven and had never had a woman." The look on his face had turned to desperation. Sweat was glistening on his forearms.

"We drove out on a country road and got out of the car."

Paul made a fist, pounded his thigh and screamed. The listeners in both rooms jumped, it had been unexpected.

"She changed her mind. I reached for her and she shook her head no. I grabbed her by the chain on her neck to pull her toward me. The chain snapped."

His bony hands were shaped like claws.

"She yelled no, held the chain in place with the one hand and caught the trinket with the other. She shoved them in her pocket. Then she cried out for her father.

"I hit her with the back of my hand. She fell, must have hit her head. I was mad and yelled for her to get up. I kicked at her legs. The fool was dead, and I'd have to hide her body. She owed me. I took her. It was good, too. I felt powerful. Throwing her body in the trunk, I drove around."

The smile on his face was sickening. The listeners hung their heads as they thought about the scene Paul had just described.

Paul closed his eyes. He had to be exhausted, but no break was offered.

Then he burst out laughing. "I thought of the perfect solution. I'd bury her at Samuel's. If her body was found, I could point to Samuel and remind them of his goings-on with a young woman years before. I could make up a story about his involvement with her and that I had seen them together. Then the community wouldn't think so much of him, and I could be a hero."

He remained quiet for so long, the police were ready to ask some questions.

Paul began to speak again. "When I heard Samuel was dying, I figured he would leave me everything. He had no one, and I'd worked for him for years. Then I wouldn't have a worry. Then the redhead showed up."

Paul's body began to relax. They gave him a few minutes.

"Did you show up at Miss Sally's when she had moved into the cottage?"

Paul sneered. "Sure."

"What happened to the kitten?"

Paul shrugged his shoulders. The policeman left it at that. Then the officer began asking him about the other happenings.

Paul tilted his head and stared at the man. "I have no idea what you're talking about." Coming up with a thought, he said, "Sounds like tricks Vera would pull."

"Vera?"

"Met her late last fall down at Billie's Bar. She was hanging out at my place when I thought I was going to be able to offer her an old mansion she could fix up and we'd be somebody.

"Then we met Smitty. Vera talked him into keeping us informed about schedules and changes during the big overhaul. She was tired of me and started camping out with him."

This new information had Sally hopping out of her chair. Immediately one of the men moved to the interrogation room and tapped on the door. A recess was called. Paul was allowed to smoke.

Everyone was looking at Sally. "What?"

"Smitty has been my main man. He's not really in charge at the house, but he's dependable, and we've talked many times about details. No wonder our progress was so well known.

"That's not all. Since Paul has been in police custody, Smitty's been gone."

She had trusted him. She had to admit Webster was right. Not all humans are good guys.

Chapter 33

When the week was ending, the police picked up Vera and Smitty in a neighboring state.

Sally was asked if she was going to press charges. She decided not to. It was suggested that they move on and change their ways. Their information was in the local office files should there be any future trouble.

Everyone was relieved that Paul had confessed. A trial would have been lengthy, and the town had had enough notoriety.

Paul explained that he'd stashed the car because he was afraid to sell it, fearing that some piece of evidence would be discovered.

Instead of the incident erasing itself in time, the car became a living being. Sometimes, when he opened the side door, he swore that he could feel the girl's heartbeat vibrating in his own body.

Once he was sure he heard her call her father's name. He'd locked the door and raced for the house. That's when he began to frequent Billie's Bar. He was glad it was over. Maybe there would be some help for him at the prison.

Web explained to Sally that Paul would be imprisoned, on open manslaughter, and spend the rest of his life locked up.

He had told Webster his only regret was losing the freedom to create beauty with the plants from the nursery. That was the one thing that had brought him happiness. He mentioned no sorrow for the young life he had taken.

Webster summoned Sally to his office on August first.

"The nursery business reverts back to you. I asked the employees if one of them would like to take it over. No luck. You'll have to decide what to do."

Sally shook her head. "One thing, Paul worked hard to build it into what it is today. He deserves the acknowledgment of his success. Can we set up a small fund to cover any minor needs he might have?"

"I'll take care of that. I hope he appreciates your generosity."

"Because of the situation there will be an abundance of paperwork to straighten everything out. I'd suggest you get on with this as soon as possible."

Sally spent the afternoon walking the beach and listening to the water wash up on the shore.

Having no idea as to the hiring of a nursery manager, she walked into the kitchen of the big house. Taking a piece of notebook paper, she compiled a letter.

Tim,

I know you're busy and have little spare time but, man, I need some help.

I'm assuming you know of ongoing situations here from the newspapers. I can clue you in on details and truth.

I need a nursery manager and have no idea what to look for in such a position. Could you draw up some guidelines for me? I'll be happy to pay a fee for your assistance.

— Sal

It was Sunday morning early. Sally was sitting in her swing on the cottage porch. She felt lazy. She was still wrapped in her bathrobe and watching the steam rise from her mug of hazelnut coffee. The aroma was wonderful, almost as good as the taste.

Watching a car kicking up dust the length of the drive did not disturb her feeling of complacency. The trucks and heavy equipment had destroyed the paving. When finished it would be replaced.

When the car ground to a stop, that good feeling evaporated. The driver was out his door instantly. Obviously, his anger had been gathering steam for some time.

"Well, how much are you going to pay me for my advice, Miss Money Bags?"

Another sip of coffee, but now it tasted like witchhazel.

"I'm sorry, Tim. I needed to turn to someone."

"I was pleased, believe me, until you offered me money. I thought we were old friends. Sure I can help.

"I think your brain has turned into a watermelon. The seeds are money, and you need to learn how to spit them out."

Tim slowed down long enough to look at Sally's face. She was like a small child who had been severely reprimanded and didn't know why.

He still felt hurt, but now he had hurt back.

Opening the screen door, he sat next to her on the swing. Taking the mug from her hand, he set it on the little round table.

"Why didn't you call me? I'd have been here in a flash. You know, like Flash Gordon in the comic books." They were laughing and crying at the same time and clinging to each other.

"I'm sorry, Sal."

Sally put her head on Tim's shoulder and told him what had been taking place.

"Then I come along and jump all over you, some pal."

The swing rocked slowly back and forth and, for a few minutes, Sally dozed off. Tim kissed her on the forehead; that's what woke her up, but she missed the touching gesture. "I didn't expect you to come by."

"Well, I'm here. How about getting dressed. Then we can go by the nursery so I can see what kind of a manager you need."

With a big sigh Sally rose. When she reached the door, she turned back. "I'm glad you're here."

Tim jotted down numerous notes at the nursery. "Can I buy you some lunch? I promise to mind my manners. I know I don't deserve it but could you come up with a smile?"

Dropping her off at the cottage, Tim said he'd go home and spend some time with his thoughts and get back to her.

When he drove by Webster's he spotted him in the yard moving sprinklers around. Stopping to talk to him for a minute changed everything.

Tim didn't know much about Webster, and he wasn't sure why he pulled over. Maybe just to get his mind on something other than the nursery business.

Mr. Webster asked him if he had some time he could spare. What difference would a few minutes make?

A few minutes turned into a few hours. There were lots of words exchanged. Legal papers were spread all over the dining room table. More talk. Tim ended up in a fitful sleep on the man's sofa. At daybreak he was fed oatmeal and juice. They shook hands and Tim headed to Lansing and his job.

It was midweek when Web heard from Tim. He called Sally and asked if she'd come to his office again.

As soon as she arrived he explained that there was a client interested in the nursery, not as a manager but as an owner.

Sally made a face. "Wow! Gosh, what do you think, Web?"

"There are lots of details to be worked out, but that way it would be set up as it was before. It would remain separate from what you are dealing with."

"Whew. Sounds good."

"Do you want me to go ahead with it then?"

"Sure, you handle it. I'm positive that you wouldn't sell to the wrong person. I'll let Tim know that everything is set. He'll be surprised. I hope he won't be put out with me after asking for his help."

Webster hoped his theory was wise.

Just before Sally closed the door he called out, "By the way, no need for funds for Paul. He never did any traveling or spent much of the money he earned. So he's covered. You can mark him off your worry list."

CHAPTER 34

Sally felt safe in having the pickup truck delivered. It was loads of fun driving around town, giving people rides. It was her celebration after the clouds that had hung over the estate. She hadn't realized how much pressure she had been under. The freedom was glorious.

On Friday, she pulled into the nursery parking area to see how things were progressing. One of the help called her over. "Hey, Sally, come have some coffee. One of the girls made a welcome cake for our new boss. Here he comes now."

Sally was stupefied. She shook her head and looked again. It couldn't be.

"He said you'd be surprised."

Sally laughed at the word surprised. "Yes, indeed."

"You want to come in the office, Miss Sally? I'll get your cake and coffee."

Sally was rubbing her forehead in disbelief when Tim shut the door.

"Shall I start at the beginning?" He explained the details, including the fact that he had a sizeable down payment and had wanted to do something on his own.

Sally locked her fingers behind her head, leaned back, and sat looking at him.

"Amazing, all this happened fast."

"Your cake and coffee."

"Sure." She began to eat the chocolate cake. "Any cream?" Tim pushed a small jar of powdered creamer toward her.

"I feel like a fool. I never bothered to ask who was interested. I was just glad to get it settled. Now I can enjoy concentrating on what I should be doing. Well, I'd better get at it."

With that she stood, reached to shake Tim's hand, and walked back to the truck.

The beach, she'd better hit the beach. This would take some thinking. Later, when she turned back toward the house she saw Webster coming her way.

"Thought I'd better find you. Did I do the wrong thing?"

"Probably not. I'm just confused. Life is moving fast. I can't seem to keep up."

Web linked his arm with hers. They came upon a good sitting log. No words, just understanding. They shared the sounds of the lake and the cool breeze.

"I'm grilling burgers tonight. Want to join me? You could stop and pick up some potato salad, get the kind that says it's like Grandma used to make." They were both laughing and Sally was feeling better. "Then for dessert we can go to the creamery, and I'll buy you your chocolate ice cream with two peanut butter cups."

"Webster you're a peach. Then tomorrow I can wake up and start anew. Let's do it."

The following day Sally called Lois, then went to her office to spend time with her. There was a lot to talk over.

Lois assured her that all bills were being paid on time.

"I don't know how I could manage without you. You deserve a raise." Lois smiled. She hadn't thought about that. It was discussed and decided upon, and her smile grew even bigger. "Write that up so it's official. I'm taking you to lunch, and the rest of the afternoon is yours. My communication skills have suffered lately. We need to set up a day a week to go over things."

The next week Sally was consumed with details and possible plans for different rooms. She was also working on long-range plans for the outbuildings.

The last Monday of the month she gave Celia a call. Could she come by again, only this time she'd be under contract. Yes, she'd come. It wouldn't hurt her business at all if, when the estate was completed, her name was mentioned as assisting in the decoration.

"But," her voice was curt, "if you mention money again, I'll withdraw my offer."

Sally was embarrassed, and she didn't like watermelon. She felt that if you ask professional people to help, it was insulting not to offer to pay. Maybe she did need to practice spitting seeds.

Celia spoke again. "I'm delighted that you've considered my advice. It's like a vacation for me."

"I've got ideas but I'm not sure how to make them come about." It was decided that Celia would arrive on Thursday.

Sally ran into Web downtown and mentioned that Celia would be around toward the end of the week. He laughed and winked at her. "Thursday, right?

"She called. Has her room at the motel. When you're not working her hard, I asked her to spend time with me. I enjoy her company."

As Sally turned the corner, she ran into Jerry. He asked if she'd seen the poster for the last summer dance in the park. Her reply had been that she'd seen it but hadn't given it much thought. The week was going to be a tough one.

"I just wondered if you'd like to go with an escort."

"I think I'd be better off playing it by ear." She touched his arm. "But thanks a lot. If I decide to go, I'll just head out on my own."

Celia was free, so she came on Wednesday. When Sally woke up Thursday morning, Celia was sitting on her front porch ready to go to work.

"It would be easy to just sit here and let the day roll by. Maybe have some iced tea, scones . . ."

"How about cold cereal and juice and get to work instead?"

Celia made a face. "You were more fun when you were little, Sally. Then you wanted to play all the time." By eight o'clock, they were standing in the entryway of the big house. Sally motioned for Celia to sit on a step of the beautiful winding staircase.

Sally paced back and forth in front of her. "The house itself—I love the entryway and its staircase. Enhance it but don't change it much. There's something about it, it's elegant but not overpowering. The kitchen is as modern as they come.

"The Samuel Mansfield Library is to be left as is. It can be used with great care."

"Miz Lila Witherspoon's room will be on display from the doorway.

"The ballroom needs to be totally renovated. It is to be functional and absolutely perfect.

"The other bedrooms and whatever are to be comfortable, not foolishly fancy. No hot tubs or that kind of stuff."

"But . . . ," Celia said.

Sally interrupted Celia. "No! If they need that let them go somewhere else. True love does not need such gadgets.

"Naturally the dining room and living room have to be completely done over."

Wearily, Sally sat down next to Celia, who remained quiet for some time. Then she slid closer and put her arm around Sally's shoulder. By doing so, she discovered that Sally was crying. "What is it, child?"

"Someday, some nice young man will truly love me, that's for sure." With that Sally jumped up and ran out the front door.

Celia sat there trying to sort out something, and she had no idea where to begin.

Ten minutes or so later, Sally returned. "I'm sorry, I'm tired, I guess."

Celia asked, "Exactly what are your plans for this place?"

"It could be so lovely. What a fine place for someone special to be married. It could be inside or outside. Close friends or family members could stay over a day or so in preparation. After the reception, it would only be occupied by the bride and groom: for the wedding night, or the honeymoon."

"Well, my soul, our little Sally is a romantic."

"I've tried to hide it." With that she laughed.

"When some of my ideas for the outbuildings are finished, there will be variations. What do you think?"

"Marvelous. Do you get to check out the couple to see if it's the real thing?"

"I'm not sure I can get away with that."

"Where did you come up with this?"

"It just seemed like a natural. I'd like to put in some kind of waterfall, outside and inside. The place is large enough. The staircase, can't you picture the bride in her flowing gown?"

"Well, we've got a big job here. I may have to move this way to make sure you do it right."

"Is that the only reason?" Sally moved quickly so Celia couldn't reach her. "I'd allow older couples to marry at reduced rates." She jumped to her feet and beat Celia to the door.

They were both laughing and chasing each other in the yard when Charlotte pulled up.

"Straighten up, Celia. Act your age. You are embarrassing me."

"What are you girls up to?"

Neither dared to explain. "We are goofing off instead of working, and there must be five years' worth of work to do. Make this girl get serious, Charlotte."

"I came by to see if either of you is going to the dance. T.T. is hesitant. I thought if I could convince him others that he knew were going . . ."

"Web and I are planning on it."

Sally shrugged her shoulders. "I'm not sure."

Celia said, "She's going all right. She's going to put on her most fetching frock and dance with all the eligible men. We had better keep a good hold on our men, that's for sure."

It was the end of August and some of the leaves had begun to fall. Luckily, it was a warm evening so they didn't have to move the dance inside somewhere. They had decorated with green and gold. You could see the lights from blocks away. It seemed like the whole town was turning out for the festivities. The committee had acquired a pretty good band. There were different styles of music so everyone could dance.

Sally went over to sit with her friends from the bank. She and Tom Brown had everyone laughing when they did some funky dance routine.

Jerry had to work the dance because one of the officers was ill. He knew he wasn't supposed to dance while in uniform but Sally caught him off guard and they danced a polka.

She had gone to where Charlotte and Celia and their partners were sitting to see if they needed any cider or popcorn.

Before she got an answer, she was whirled onto the floor to dance to the number, "Can I Have This Dance for the Rest of My Life."

"Ah, Timothy, it is you."

"Don't talk. Just dance."

They did just that, for it was getting late and the band was playing smooth dance music. As the music stopped, Tim kissed Sally's hand and said, "You are beautiful." Then he turned and disappeared in the crowd.

The two older couples and Jerry observed Sally and Tim.

If they had put their thoughts into words, it would have been a clear shot from Cupid's arrow. "Why can't they admit it? All it would take is the right words from one of them."

Sally rode home with Charlotte and T.T. The car radio played something mellow. There was no exchange of words. She thanked them and entered her cottage. She felt tired, dreamy. and confused. Removing her pale blue dress, she slid into bed and a deep lazy sleep surrounded by slow waltz music.

Before Celia left for home, she called Sally. She had some additional questions about things they had discussed.

She also wanted some information on things not mentioned.

"Sally, you aren't planning on doing catering and all, that are you?"

"No, that will have to be up to the person making the arrangements. As time goes on, I hope to have suggestions and recommendations for all kinds of services.

"One thing I do have is the business card of a photographer. She's young, early twenties. The business is called 'Sadie Saturdays.' She has a full-time job, but on weekends she has developed quite a clientele.

"Her portfolio is growing. She hopes to someday have a place of her own. Maybe a small tea room where she can display her work and do her photo developing out of the back."

Celia promised to gather detailed ideas and sketches before returning.

 CHAPTER 35

September had bombarded the area with nastiness. It had chased the workers inside and some of the rooms were being transformed.

Sally began to feel like she was accomplishing her goals. Because of the size of the project, it didn't look like much, but even the tiniest detail had to be done to specification. Finishing the job incorrectly would be a disaster. Samuel had provided financial backing to have things done right. It was Sally's responsibility to see that his wishes were carried out.

With the troublemakers out of the way, she felt safe exploring the estate, even late at night.

In her yellow slicker and high rubber boots she had made her way to the big house. Every room she passed through she flicked on lights. A dark empty mansion was unhealthy for one's imagination.

The wind was whipping the cold rain against the windows. It sounded like the old shutters were being ripped off their hinges.

She hadn't decided whether to eliminate or replace them. Maybe the storm would help by demonstration.

Thunder shook the house. Hopefully, the lightning wouldn't uproot any of the ancient trees. Still nature had its reasons. Possibly, some needed to be removed.

Sally had discovered a shoebox containing letters from the past on a shelf in the closet of Miz Lila's room. Earlier in the day, she had climbed on a stool to clean the shelf and ceiling so it would be ready for the painters.

She had settled in on the floor where the light was best to read the secrets of the beautiful lady in the picture in the dining area. She wanted to move the portrait to a significant spot but hadn't figured out where.

There was a temporary lull in the storm. That's when she heard the racket.

The noise from outside had Sally grabbing her flashlight and pushing the balcony door open. Waving the beam along the base of the house, she spotted the culprit. There . . . the yellow Lab was in a panic, digging at the foundation.

As the noise of the storm increased, the dog broke through the basement window.

Sally raced to the basement. The whining noise was coming through the door that no one had been able to budge.

Running up the stairs to the kitchen, she dialed Tim's number, having no idea what time it was.

"Hello."

Sally's voice was shaky when she spoke. "Tim, it's me. Something is wrong and I need help."

"Where are you?"

"At the mansion. A dog has broken the glass to the basement window of that room that no one has been able to open. He was frightened by the storm. I have no idea what's in there. He may have been cut by the glass."

The line was disconnected.

Sally didn't know if Tim was coming or didn't want to bother on such a night.

He found her sitting on the basement stairs rocking back and forth in a muddled state.

Sally wondered how he could have gotten there so fast. Trying to clear her thinking, she realized that she didn't know where he was staying.

Tim had picked up a crowbar he'd seen in the corner of the garage where he rented.

Looking up, Sally said, "I didn't know if you'd come."

He pulled her to her feet. Scowling, he shook his head. What he wanted to do was give her a good shaking.

"Never think that if you need me that I won't help you." His eyes flashed like the lightning outside. "Do you understand?"

She nodded her head. He could hear the dog below scratching at the door. They joined hands and headed down the stairs.

Tim was using the crowbar in every way he could think of pounding, prying. Sally didn't know if his shirt was wet from the rain or sweat. They could hear the dog panting. Tim wiped his forehead. With a look of determination, he wedged the bar near the lock one more time, and the door gave way. Tim stumbled backward with the Lab on top of him.

The success gave them a pause and time to laugh. Even the dog seemed to join in. In seconds the laughter stopped. The three of them were spattered with blood.

Sally hurried up the stairs and returned with clean material that was stacked in the kitchen. It was to be used on the floors by the painters.

Tim wrapped the dog and they headed for his car. Sally sat in the back with the dog's head in her lap.

"There's a vet not far from my place who stays open evenings for emergencies."

Three bloodied creatures entered the front office. The woman rushed them into the back room, and they placed the animal on the examining table. "Was it a car accident?" Sally filled the vet in.

"Dog's name?"

Tim spoke up, "Mike."

"I'm going to give him a shot so he'll relax. I need to go over him carefully. I may need some assistance, but now I'd like you to wait in the other room."

They shut the door, and Tim stood in the middle of the room. With no hesitation, Sally leaned into him. She couldn't stop shaking. Tim wrapped his arms around her, resting his chin on the top of her head. Sally slid her arms around his waist. They were still in that position and half-asleep when the vet opened the door.

"There are lots of cuts. I could use two assistants. Go in the back and shower up. Put on some clean white cotton pants and tops hanging there."

The vet was busy with stitches. Her assistants were holding intravenous feeding tubes and handing her sterile equipment.

"Help me move him to the big padded cage. Is he your dog?"

"No."

"What's to happen to him if he recovers?"

Sally said, "I'd like to keep him, but suppose he belongs to someone?"

"Let's do this. If he pulls through I'll check around and see if he has an owner. If not, he's yours."

"I'll cover the bill."

Tim said, "Oh, no, we'll split the bill. Even if he lives at your place, he's our dog."

The smile on Sally's face was so special. Tim wanted to kiss her then and there, but he couldn't move. Holding her earlier had made his heart race.

"We'll return the whites tomorrow when we check on Mike."

After they left the office the vet grinned to herself. As she doused the lights she wasn't sure which would be more interesting, watching the dog regain his strength or the couple get themselves straightened out.

 # CHAPTER 36

On the bright and sunny Sunday of September fifteenth Tim and Sally brought Mike home. Tim had left immediately.

There was a big promotional sale going on at the nursery, mums of every color. The display work was fabulous. Tim ran a contest. Each employee entered a sketch of his idea. The prize was $100 and a day off with pay. It also gave him more information as to their capabilities.

Sally made her way to the basement room where they had rescued Mike. She had gone down several times with intention of investigating the area. For some reason each time she had backed off.

Seconds later she heard the click of Mike's nails on the stairs. The window had been replaced, but it didn't let in much light. There was no light switch in that room.

With her powerful camping lantern, she scoured every inch of the room. It was dry, the floor was dirt, and the walls were large stones with mortar in between. Several shelves were in decay by the far wall.

Mike made his way behind one of them, and Sally heard him scratching at something.

Pulling the shelf out farther from the wall, Sally could make out the outline of a small door. Hesitantly, she pulled on a piece of rope and the door slowly came open, freeing an expulsion of fumes and dust.

An unrecognizable odor slid past Sally in a graceful but formless mirage. Sally's fear had escaped also.

She wanted to reach out and touch it but was unable to move.

It faded and only the smell of the dusty basement remained.

You would have to stoop to enter. Peering into the tunnel, she saw nothing but cobwebs and emptiness.

She crouched by Mike and held his collar. "This is as far as we go, boy."

They remained as they were. She was positive that she heard . . . something. A faint whisper. The two of them raced for the stairs. Tumbling over each other repeatedly, they finally made it to the top and slammed the door.

Taking big gulps of air, Sally hugged the dog. "You're a lot of help."

It had to have been air coming through a crack somewhere along the tunnel. Calling Web she asked, "You doing anything special?"

"Nodding off from boredom."

"Well, come on over to the big house. Mike and I have something that will wake you up."

When Web arrived, they made their way down the stairs. Sally and Web carried folding chairs that they set up by the open tunnel door. Sally retrieved her lantern. Luckily it had shut off when she dropped it. She motioned for silence. Mike sat between them.

Web was ready to speak when Sally shook her head no. There it was again. She jerked her head toward Web. He was staring at her with his eyes wide.

Sally stood slowly and carefully shut the tunnel door, then the door to that room. The three of them made their way upstairs and closed that door.

Web started to speak again, and Sally put her finger to her lips. Handing him a piece of paper and a pencil, and taking the same, she spoke. "Please write down what you heard and if you saw anything." They switched papers when finished. The papers were much the same.

A whimper of a small child and a woman whispering for him to be silent.

Each took a deep breath.

"So, I'm not imagining things?"

"I won't swear to that, but we both heard something."

They sat contemplating what to do.

Sally perked up. "I'm not frightened by this, but I need answers. I think I should have searched further back into the family history, while I was at the library. It may be that they helped with the Underground Railroad on occasions.

"The more I find out about these people and this place, the more intrigued I become. My first opinion was that it was a mundane group. The true background may prove to be lively."

After sitting for a few minutes, Sally's eyes brightened. "I'm going to do what Samuel did, padlock that outer door. When I have more time, I will solve this mystery. Until then, it is our secret."

Web shook his head and laughed.

The following day Sally purchased a strong lock. She also found a couple of army cots at the surplus store.

Arriving at the house, she found sheets and blankets in a cupboard in an upstairs hallway. Plus there were two pillows with crocheted lace pillow cases.

Down the steps she went. She opened the two doors, set up the cots, and lay the linens on top in front of the open tunnel.

She could hear someone calling her from upstairs. Hurriedly, she arrived at the top step, explaining that she was organizing supplies below.

A delivery man had arrived with paint, brushes, and cleaning materials. He wanted her to sign the order and write him a check. Sally did sign, then gave him directions to the office at Lois's house.

The phone was ringing, and she caught it before the person hung up. "Pizza, who ordered pizza?"

"The work crew tearing down some dilapidated buildings at the back of the property. They used a cell phone." The pizza man wanted to make sure it was a legitimate order.

"Send it on and send the bill to the office. Tell Lois I okayed it. I'll surprise them. Send an extra tall pop for me. I'm hungry. I'll eat with them today." Sally rode back to where the workers were with the driver. This was not the usual routine, and the kid told her the boss said, Any time. She slipped him a big tip. He grinned and winked, informing her that he worked at lunch time and be sure to ask for Hank.

It was the following morning before Sally recalled what she was doing before all the interruptions.

Sally headed downstairs. Hurrying into the room, she stopped. Couldn't be. Everything was as she had left it but . . . The one pillow had an indentation as if a tiny head had rested there. One blanket looked like it had kept someone warm.

Sally backed from the room. Before closing the door, she spoke softly, "Take care. One of these days I'll be back." She snapped the new lock into place and pocketed the key.

Calling Web, she shared her experience.

"Why did you put sheets and stuff down there?"

"It's a woman thing, I guess. If people are staying over, you get out the company bedding."

The following afternoon, Sally went to the basement, determined to release the souls from the past. She unlocked the door in the basement, and the one outside. With reverence she said, "You earned your freedom long ago, God speed."

The next morning she retraced her steps. On the white pillow lay a single red rose. Locking both doors, Sally, folded the chairs and cots. She gathered the linens to be washed. The red rose was placed in a vase on Lila's dresser.

It was an experience that she would not soon forget.

 CHAPTER 37

Sally often thought about the detailed decisions she needed to make concerning the mansion.

The old window latches were unique. She'd never seen the likes. The windows would have to be scraped and painted each year.

She could save a few to show visitors. Yes, she would have to install up-to-date ones to help insulate the house.

The potting shed: she wanted it to be a charming guest room or a private spot for tea time.

Her biggest secret was she wanted the mansion to be called The Witherspoon Inn, owned by Samuel Mansfield, managed by . . .

The days and weeks were rolling by. Sally and Tim had not communicated since they brought Mike home.

The end of September had produced spectacular leaf colors. The mildness of Indian summer enveloped the area, dispersing the thoughts of the winter to follow.

Tourists were continuing to wander through the downtown shops. She was hoping to accumulate all data on this piece of land and those who called it home. Eventually, she'd put together a booklet to give each guest.

Boaters were hesitant to store their water fun equipment.

Sally threw the tennis ball and Mike raced across the lawn in pursuit.

The sun provided the feeling that all was well.

A rental car pulled up and out jumped Celia, waving her straw hat. Mike forgot the ball and rushed up to greet her. Sally strolled toward her and they exchanged hugs.

"I didn't expect you."

"I had to come. I have so much to show you. I'll get the samples from the back seat. We need to go in so they can be spread out on the table. There are sketches and photos, too."

"What have you been working on?"

Celia beamed. "I'm so excited. It's the entryway. Come and see."

Sally studied the plans. "Now explain it to me."

"The walls are painted a soft ivory, like French vanilla ice cream."

"Yum."

"Oh, stop. Get serious. The handrail and spindles are dark. The stairs are carpeted in bright red. There is a fabulous chandelier that can be dimmed. A large mirror surrounded by an ornate gold frame. Rich red carpeting with intricate designs covered the floor."

Celia collapsed on a kitchen chair.

"You are wound up tight."

"I can see this, and I hope you are as satisfied as I am." She barely paused before continuing. "I also called the lady in the library, and we discovered some additional information."

That had Sally leaning forward.

"You know that exquisite close-up painting of the rose?"

"The one in Miz Lila's room?"

"Years back, the local garden club had a contest. Miz Lila won. The perfect rose was displayed and next to it was a replica of it in the painting."

"Did Samuel grow the rose and she painted it?"

"No one knew, but the blue ribbon went to Lila. I'd like to see that in the entry and also the portrait of the lady."

Sally snapped her fingers. "I agree."

Celia started off again. "At the back, a large glass door with a beveled edge looking out to the gardens. Inside, near that area, a small gurgling fountain with shaded lighting."

Celia was out of breath and bursting with excitement, but questions were still rolling out of her mouth.

"What was in the room in the basement? What did you find in the shoebox of letters in Lila's room? Did you get the okay for this project you are wanting to establish on this property?"

"Stop it! Are you having a heart attack or something? I'll not answer your questions until you've had some rest and quieted down. Your ideas are fabulous. Go rest. Can I reach you at the motel?"

"No!"

Sally waited.

"I've been invited to stay at Webster's." With that Celia gathered her things, took a deep breath, and walked to her car. Slowly, she drove to the gate.

Sally stood there a long time. Was this good or bad? Poor Celia was unstrung.

Later that evening, Sally dialed Web's number. His hello was so heavy with sadness, she hesitated in asking about Celia.

"Could I speak with Celia, please?"

"I don't know. She's in her room crying."

"Web, please, take your portable phone to the door and tell her I insist." Sally listened intently but got no clue as to the trouble. She could hear sniffles and nose blowing.

"Hey, what's going on over there?" More blubbering, and then hiccups. She didn't dare laugh. "You better come clean with me."

Through chokes and sobs, Celia finally got the words out. "Web asked me to marry him."

Sally nearly fell off her chair. "Do you love him?"

More blubbering. "Yes, of course I do."

"I'm going to hang up. You're going to hang up. Splash some cold water on your face, then march your petite body in there and tell him yes." By the end of the message, Sally was shouting. She slammed the receiver down.

 CHAPTER 38

In the morning, Sally was still feeling guilty about the way she had spoken to Celia. Feeling embarrassed, she dialed Web's number. When he answered, he sounded different from the previous day.

Timidly, she asked if she could speak to Celia.

"You mean the future Mrs. Webster?"

"What! Oh, Web, I'm so happy for each of you. I'll talk to her another time. Congratulations."

Hanging up the phone, she called for Mike. "Come on boy, we must celebrate. A romp along the water will be good for us."

They ran until Sally was out of breath and Mike's tongue was hanging out of the side of his mouth. Then they rested. Sally laughed and Mike looked like he was doing the same.

Jumping up, they chased each other and rolled in the sand.

Finding a perfect spot in the dunes that was protected from the wind Sally sat down to watch the wave pattern. Mike snuggled up beside her.

"Good old Mike. You're a sweetheart." As much as she loved the dog, thoughts ran through her mind. Wouldn't it be nice to have a young man sharing this moment? She ruffled the hair on Mike's head. "You're a good boy."

Rising, she brushed the sand from her clothes as best she could.

It was time to head back. The undertow had coaxed her laughter out to deeper water.

Nothing was planned for the balance of the day so they lazed around. It was beginning to get dark so Sally put her pajamas on. She sat watching the news.

"Well, Mike, we took the day off. Our fling at exercise seems to have done us in."

Mike came to stiff attention, cocking his head, listening. He began to pace back and forth. Going by the back door, he began to whine.

"You were just out. Oh, no!" Something was on fire at the back of the property. Sally dialed 911, then slid into her jeans, sweat shirt, and tennis shoes.

The door was barely open when Mike almost knocked her down. He was off like a shot.

Sally was close behind him. It was back by the big lake. Toward the house, all that could be seen was a large mound of dirt and grass. On the lake side, years ago someone had built a storage shed that backed into the mound. She and the men had been going to dismantle it and level the dirt to get rid of the eyesore. There was more wood than she realized. The flames were high. The crackling sound scared her because there were still dead leaves on the ground. The crew from the nursery had said they would clear them out the following week.

Mike was desperately sniffing the ground. Sally heard the fire trucks and a police car. Mike began to bark. She followed the sound that was coming from the opposite side of the fire. A man was on the ground writhing and crying out in pain.

Sally ran back where the firemen were working. It was then she spotted a rescue unit pulling in. She waved her arms so they'd follow her.

They jumped from their vehicle, grabbing their medical bags, and ran to the man.

"His hands are burned." As they were working on him Sally heard them talking. "It's old Walter again. You've done things up good this time, old pal. We'll get you to the hospital, hang on, old buddy. Don't be frightened."

Mike tried to jump into the unit. "No, fella, you can't ride along.

"I think that was the dog that was hanging around last time Walter got into a jam."

"You're right. I'd forgotten."

The policeman came over to talk to the two men before they left.

The firemen were putting away their hoses. "Miss, we're going to recommend that a hydrant be put close to this place. If the fire had gotten out of hand, we might have had trouble containing it."

The police car was pulling away. Sally ran after it and knocked on the window. The policeman rolled the window down. "Wait, can someone tell me exactly what took place here? I've been thanking everyone but I'm puzzled."

The officer stepped out and smiled. "I'm sorry. We solved the immediate problem but got a big zero on public relations."

"Walter is homeless . . . and a bit . . . slow. He makes mistakes. We take him to shelters, he stays a few days and off he goes." He shook his head. "Those hands will keep him in the hospital for a while. Then I don't know."

"What was he doing here?"

"My guess is he's been here a while. He finds a place he likes and sticks around for as long as no one spots him."

"I heard one of the men mention that this dog was with him last time he had difficulty. Come to think of it, Mike has been out of sight a lot the last week or so."

The officer sighed. "Two homeless people, I guess. I apologize again for not keeping you informed."

Sally patted Mike's head. "So, you two are friends. Then we'll have to do something about this."

"Does anyone have an idea of what started the fire, Officer?"

"Walt said he'd trapped a rabbit and wanted to cook it inside so no one would spot the blaze. It got out of control. He tried to put it out with his hands. The smoke chased him outside."

Sally was almost in tears. Mike was leaning against her leg.

"Mike and I will make periodic visits while Walter's hospitalized. Then I'd like someone to find a suitable place where he'd like it well enough to stay. I will cover the cost, and Mike and I will visit on a regular basis. Who should I see about that?"

The officer stared at Sally, then turned away. When he turned again, Sally was surprised by the way he looked.

"Officers are not supposed to get emotional while on duty." He handed her a slip of paper with the name of the person to contact.

Then he extended his hand. "It's been nice meeting you."

As he drove away he waved out the window.

Two days later, Sally and Mike entered the hospital. Walking up to the information desk, she asked where a man named Walter was being cared for.

"The man with the burns. You can't see him. He's in a glassed-in room to protect him from infection."

"Could I speak to someone about this, please?"

A head nurse was rounding the corner. She had overheard the conversation. The hair on the back of her neck bristled. Her body stiffened and she glared at them. She said nothing.

Sally smiled. "Could I speak to you privately for just a moment?"

The nurse stared her down. "There are rules and there are reasons for them." But she did oblige Sally by moving away from the desk.

Sally shared the whole story with her. "We would be very careful and would only disturb him for a minute."

"I thought maybe if he saw the dog it might give him a reason to hope."

The nurse turned and stared out the window for a long time. Then she motioned with her head for them to follow.

"The pain is terrible when someone is burned. There isn't much we can do but give them shots so they sleep. He had just rung for some relief. I'll let him see the dog through the glass then I'll take care of him."

Walter looked up; Sally had Mike put his paws on the outside of the glassed area.

"He's wagging his tail, Walter. Says he wants you to get well."

Walter's eyes teared up and he smiled. The nurse moved in, and Sally and Mike left immediately.

Two more days passed and the two of them returned. The young woman at the desk hurried out to them. "Walter died in his sleep last night. I hoped someone had let you know. He was old and didn't take good care of himself. It must have been too much for his system to handle.

"The nurse told me that yesterday he repeatedly asked if 'his dog' really did come to visit him."

Sally looked like she was going to faint. The girl helped her to a chair. "Are you okay?"

"I'll be fine." She shook her head. "I feel like a collapsed balloon. I'm sorry, boy. Your friend didn't make it." Mike hugged up next to her leg. Sally got the name of the funeral parlor.

A gentleman met her at the door. Sally inquired into the arrangements for such a person as Walter but was not happy with what she heard.

"That dog should not be in here."

Sally's chin shot up, and she acted as sophisticated as possible. Nodding at Mike, she claimed, "He was Walter's friend. I'm just helping him with alternative arrangements."

She was sure she could see the man's eyes light up with dollar signs.

"Of course."

All of a sudden, he was Mr. Congeniality.

"This is what we want: he's to have comfortable pants. It's going to be cold soon, so a warm flannel shirt and slippers."

"Right."

"A decent casket, nothing fancy. He's to be buried at the back of the cemetery by a nice tree. If he gets tired of the box, he can lean against the trunk. You got that?"

"Yes, Madam. We'll take care of it."

"I know you will, because tomorrow I will come by to check everything out before you close the lid. Then Mike and I will ride with you to the cemetery." She smiled. "Don't call me Madam. Figure the bill and I will write you a check."

On the way home, Sally told Mike that she thought they had done the proper thing.

That night was the one time when Mike was allowed to sleep next to Sally.

 CHAPTER 39

Sally was delighted. Charlotte and T.T. had been planning their bike trip for more than a month. Two months before, their current instructor of the weekly armchair travel class had decided to get real.

According to T.T., the man had surprised the group by suggesting a two-week bike trip through the Netherlands. None of them had dreamed of doing such a thing. T.T. said the teacher claimed he had expected enthusiasm or excitement, not complete silence.

The room might as well have been empty. T.T. said, "I couldn't hear anyone breathing."

Someone in the back row had begun to cry. Then he heard her say, "Do you think I could really do something like that? I've never been on a vacation on my own."

Everyone started talking. Mr. Stilwell gave a sigh of relief. He assured them the trip would be geared for them so it would be something they could enjoy.

Charlotte, T.T., and Sally had said their good-byes the evening before, when Sally had them over for dinner. It was then that she had found out that they were leaving early so they could visit Charlotte's two sons and their families. They would fly out on their own and meet the group in Amsterdam.

T.T. was the only one transporting his bike. The others would rent theirs. They had been assured that they would avoid the larger cities.

When Sally arrived at the mansion the following noon she went to fix a peanut butter sandwich, grab a few chips and some grape soda.

The floors above were buzzing with workers. She had put her lunch on an old tray she'd salvaged from the dump pile. After a good cleaning it was usable.

As she closed the door to the library. she immediately felt the quiet surround her. Many times she had been sure that Samuel had joined her here. That's why she never sat in his chair. She watched the lake while she ate.

After finishing she walked to the shelves and picked up their favorite book. ready to turn to page 652. She was going to read "The Raven" out loud. All these months she hadn't laid her hand on the book. A piece of paper fluttered to the floor. Reaching to pick it up she found it to be folded in half. She didn't remember leaving anything to mark that page. Opening it she was astonished. Quickly she moved to the window.

Sally, my girl, where have you been I've been waiting here for you. I hope things are going well. So, you have found me at last. One more surprise. You will have to look for it. It's by the waterway. There's a place I call Turtle Creek. It's hidden, but worth the search. Meet you there. Samuel

What a rascal.

Her heart was racing as she stepped to the back door. It had started to sprinkle. Charlotte stood there ready to knock. "One more quick hug. You look flushed, are you okay?"

To reassure her that all was well, Sally smiled. They hugged each other then Sally said, "A strange thing has happened and I must check it out. Have a marvelous trip. I've got to go." She turned and ran toward the channel.

It was early October, the Indian Summer was appreciated. It gave a person a chance to breathe deep and catch the smells of autumn. It was enough to confuse your planned wardrobe. Even the light rain was comfortable. Each day held back the chills of winter.

When Charlotte returned home Tim was talking to T.T. "I've come to wish you a safe journey. Were you saying good-bye to your wealthy neighbor who owns the castle yonder?"

Charlotte's smile disappeared. "Why would you talk like that? You should be ashamed."

Tim felt like she had belted him in the stomach. His look of bewilderment softened her to some degree. "I refuse to let you two pull out of this driveway on a sour note. What's the problem?"

"You."

"I don't get it."

"Why don't you marry that girl."

"Why? I'm afraid to ask her." Charlotte was going to say something when he stopped her. "Wait. Last Christmas, Samuel asked me the same question. I've loved her since I met her years ago. Samuel says, don't let her get away. Promise me you'll take care of her. Then he dies and leaves her a fortune. What do I have to offer her?"

T.T. didn't want to interfere but he couldn't hold back. "You might offer her the love you are carrying around."

"That's not enough."

"Are you sure? Maybe you should talk it over with her."

Charlotte said, "I think I may be able to give you some advice. After Samuel died she and I used to talk about this 'little rich girl' halo hanging over her head. She told me that she didn't think of herself as rich. She had just taken on a different job. She hasn't purchased anything for herself."

Tim grabbed her and gave her a bear hug.

"Hey, where's mine?" T.T. asked.

"No time to spare, I've got to find Sally."

"Last time I saw her she was heading toward the channel."

Tim sprinted away.

T.T. smiled at Charlotte and kissed her on the forehead. "These young folks waste a lot of time. By the way, you look lovely today."

Charlotte nudged his arm with her elbow and wrinkled her nose. "Let's go."

All Tim could think of was, I have to find Sally, now.

Sally had come upon hedges and trees that blocked her from going any further. She knew how to get to the channel from the road but getting through this seemed impossible. She stood still and listened intently. Hearing water gurgling over stones had her walking up and down the barrier again. There, it would be a squeeze and she'd get scratched up. It was as if the water was repeatedly murmuring, Come, come and see.

Sally got tangled in some thorn bushes, but what she saw on the other side was fascinating.

Turtle Creek didn't amount to much, but it was enough to float a miniature houseboat. The creek was more wide than deep. The soft slap of the water against the flat-bottom barge sounded inviting.

There was a boarding plank. She stepped carefully on it and pulled the rope that opened the door. There was a musty odor. On a small table sat a white envelope. Mice had nibbled at one corner. Her name was printed across the front by an unsteady hand.

She sat for a few minutes on a bench. Her courage returned and she opened the envelope carefully.

My dearest Sally,

This was my hideaway. You can use it for that or whatever you like. I often came here to read.

One year on the parade of homes they had a houseboat you could view. It was tied up at Block Lake. I had no intention of looking through fancy houses. I bought my ticket and made sure I was the first visitor. I didn't want to wrestle with others. I have enclosed pictures I took.

They were curled and bent but Sally looked through them.

The photos beaconed you to come aboard. There were white railed porches front and back, flower boxes and hanging baskets. Windows everywhere including over the kitchen sink. It had a small comfortable sitting area, a mounted TV and phone. A special refrigerator and freezer tall but slender. There was a stove built into the countertop, and microwave, considerable cupboard and drawer space. A nice bedroom and closets, and a full bath.

I knew I couldn't duplicate it. Gradually I gathered supplies. I often wondered if anyone knew about Turtle Creek. It didn't show up on survey maps.

Gradually I built what I thought would suffice. It looked like a children's toy.

It's large enough for an adult to sit and have a cup of coffee. The bunk is comfortable if a nap is needed. (Imagine the mattress needs replacing now).The roof is good. It's a perfect quiet place for a dreamer, away from the world.

May you continue to spread sunshine.

Samuel

Sally sat on a stool with her elbows resting on the table, resting her head in her hands. It would have been easy to let the tears flow.

Then she heard someone calling her name. She shook her head.

Tim was searching for a path through the thick underbrush. Sally could barely see his silhouette. She began calling to him, guiding him to the breakaway spot.

He was brushing loose twigs off of his pants and shirt.

When he looked up Sally was smiling at him.

"Hi there."

"What do we have here?"

"A secret hideout. Another Samuel Surprise. Come aboard it's really nifty. Needs a bit of serious scrubbing."

Stepping on the wet rickety plank he slid on some moss, lost his balance, and tumbled into the creek.

Sally was doubled over with laughter but she reached out with her hand and tried to help him up.

Taking hold of it he gleefully pulled her in beside him. Holding her tight he began kissing her. When she stopped thrashing in the shallow creek and began responding he released her.

"Sally, I love you with all my heart. Marry me." She stared at him and kept shaking her head.

"Don't tell me that's a no after all this trouble I've gone to great lengths to be romantic."

Although the air was still warm, that did not spread to the creek. Neither could speak because of chattering teeth. Both stood up shivering. Sally grabbed his hand and they ran for the cottage.

They deposited their wet clothes just outside the back door, scurried in and jumped in the shower until they could stop shaking. Sally stepped out and wrapped a big fluffy towel around herself and laid one out for Tim.

Opening her closet she got out two pair of sweat pants and tops. After donning hers she warmed some water for cocoa.

As they sat at the table with their hands wrapped around the warm mugs, Sally felt numb. "Well, Sir Galahad, where have you been, what's got into you? Are you delirious?"

"No. Did you ever play Simon Says?"

"When I was a kid, sure."

"Well, I want to play Samuel Says." He repeated his story that he had shared with Charlotte. "I liked you the first time I met you. The feelings grew so strong over the years but it never seemed like the right time to express my feelings. Then the money thing scared me off big time. I never knew how you felt."

"You've been avoiding me."

"That was the easy way out. Samuel has been pushing me around a lot lately. So, I finally asked the question. Are you brave enough to answer me?"

"I do have a 'child' named Mike, you know."

"I have no problem with that. Please say yes. I can't take this situation much longer."

Sally folded her arms in front of her. "There's a lot of things we should talk about first."

"Just say yes. Then we'll talk."

Sally took Tim's face in her hands, looked into his eyes and began to kiss him. The message was clear though no words were spoken.

About the Author

As a young girl Donna Bocks wrote poetry emulating her beloved Auntie. While in college her oral storytelling was popular with roommates—"tell us a story" was the constant request. When her children arrived, Donna loved to rock them in the rocking chair and sing original story-songs spun from their everyday lives. Her literary impulses were piqued by an author interview. Afterward she realized that she could actually write down the stories in her head.

Most of Donna's novels are set in Michigan where she was born 78 years ago. "Stories happen," says Donna, "walking everyday in the neighborhood. The houses begin to speak and the stories grow street by street, house by house." Donna's oldest son asked her to take him on a walk and point out the elements of one of her novels. He was delighted as street names became names of characters, and as his familiar surroundings were sprinkled with his mother's magic storytelling dust!

The author welcomes correspondence from her readers:
P. O. Box 8231, Holland, Michigan 49422-8231
DonnaBocks@birthAbook.com

About the Illustrator

Tom Ball has always loved to draw. He studied art and architectural drawing throughout high school. To relieve the intensity of his chosen profession in law enforcement, he draws. When the family goes camping, he sketches, and his daughter does too. Tom is a two-time Olympian, having served on security details at both the Atlanta and Salt Lake City Olympics. He is the husband of Colleen, father of Travis and Sarah, and proud walker of Aspen, an English Springer Spaniel.